FEATURING MOBILE, IOT & IIOT

EDGE COMPUTING

Simply In Depth

AJIT SINGH

Copyrighted Material

Edge Computing Simply In Depth

Copyright © 2019 by Ajit Singh., All Rights Reserved.

No part of this publication may be reproduced, stored in a retrieval system or transmitted, in any form or by any means — electronic, mechanical, photocopying, recording or otherwise— without prior written permission from the author, except for the inclusion of brief quotations in a review.

For information about this title or to order other books and/or electronic media, contact the publisher:

Ajit Singh
ajit_singh24@yahoo.com
https://www.ajitvoice.in
Library of Congress Control Number: (N/A)

Preface

Edge computing for the Internet of Things (IoT) allows IoT deployments to be enhanced through data processing closer to the end device. This results in lower latency and improved efficiencies in data transport.

> IoT edge computing is significantly different from non-IoT edge computing, with distinct demands and considerations. IoT devices typically have limited data processing and storage capabilities, so substantial data processing needs to occur off the device, with the edge offering an environment to undertake this processing and manage large volumes of IoT devices and data. This, in turn, can reduce device cost, as many functions can be off-loaded to the edge. The location of the edge itself has various possibilities and will differ according to the use case. For example, the edge for IoT could reside at an operator's local or regional data centre, at a base station or at a dedicated server on the customer's premises.

IoT market analysts expect the edge to play a significant role in supporting IoT implementations going forward, as it creates efficiencies and scale in networks that makes IoT deployments more self-sustaining. IDC (International Data Corporation) estimates that by 2022, IT spending on edge infrastructure will reach up to 18 percent of the total spend on IoT infrastructure. Mobile operators have the demonstrable capability to manage infrastructure, data and applications for IoT services, and are well placed to continue this with edge for IoT.

This book features Edge Computing with respect to Mobile, IoT and IIoT technologies from evolution, architecture, implementation and standard role of IoT. All aspects have been covered with in-depth real-life and practical use cases from industry. This book covers the curriculum of the Edge Computing course at prominent global Universities / Institutions.

Acknowledgements

I would like to thank all the people who have helped me put together this book. Most of all, I would like to thank you, the reader, for trusting me to help you learn about Edge Computing.

About the Author

Ajit Singh is Assistant Professor in the Department of Computer Application, Patna Women's College, Patna, Bihar. He holds the titles of Online World Record (OWR) and Future Kalams Book of Records.

Ajit is a Ph.D. candidate at Patliputra University, Bihar. He is working on 'Social Media Predictive Data Analytics' at A. N. College Research Centre, Patna. He also holds M.Phil. Degree in Computer Science and is a Microsoft MCSE / MCDBA / MCSD.

Ajit has two decades of extensive teaching experience in Under Graduate and Post Graduate courses of Computer Science across several colleges of Patna University and NIT Patna, Bihar.

Ajit holds memberships in a number of associations including Internet Society - Delhi/Trivendrum Chapters, IEEE, International Association of Engineers, Eurasia Research, IoT Council, Python Software Foundation, Data Science Association, etc.

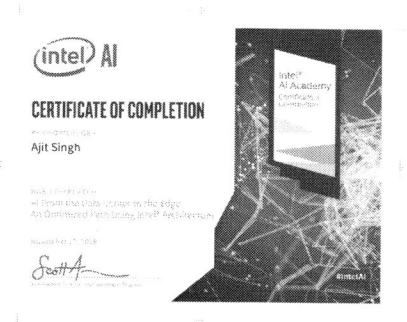

Table of Contents

Chapter 1. Introduction   06
      Edge Computing
      Concept
      Basic Characteristics and Attributes
      Edge and Real-Time
      Network Edge
      Benefits of Edge Computing
      "CROSS" Value of Edge Computing
      Collaboration of Edge Computing and Cloud Computing
      Fog and Edge Computing
      Use cases of Edge Computing
      Drawbacks of Edge Computing

Chapter 2. The Evolution of Computing Models towards Edge Computing   21
      Shared and central resources versus exclusive and local computation
      IoT disrupts the cloud
      Characteristics of the new computing model
      Blueprint of edge computing intelligence
      Definition and high level architecture
      Key Drivers of Edge Computing
      Application areas

Chapter 3. Mobile-Edge Computing   27
      Mobile cloud computing
      Cloudlets
      Mobile-Edge computing

Chapter 4. Edge Computing Reference Architecture   32
      Model-Driven Reference Architecture
      Multi-View Display
      Concept View
      ECNs, Development Frameworks, and Product Implementation
      Edge Computing Domain Models
      Function View
      ECN
      Service Fabric
      CCF
      Development Service Framework (Smart Service)
      Deployment Operation Service Framework (Smart Service)
      Management Service
      Full-Lifecycle Data Service
      Security Service
      Deployment View

Chapter 5. Edge Computing in the IoT   52
      Introduction

Where is the Mobile Operator IoT Edge?
Key Benefits of Edge for the IoT
Unique Requirements of Edge for the IoT
Use Cases for IoT Edge
IoT Foundation
Device Management
Security
Service Enablement
Message Prioritisation
Data Replication
Cloud Enablement
IoT Solutions
IoT Image and Audio Processing

Chapter 6. Standards and Role of Open Source   72
Standards for self-organization, self-configuration, self-discovery
Trust/ decentralized trust
Credible information
E/W communication Standards between multiple ECNs
Containerization Standard for embedded systems
Open standard for implementation of algorithms for machine learning
Comprehensive standard tackling carrier mode selection in case of loss of connectivity
Role of open source

Chapter 7. IIoT using Edge Computing   76
Introduction
Use Cases Industry Oriented
Technical Analytics

References   88

Chapter 1.
Introduction - Edge Computing

Concept

Historically, network architectures and computing models have oscillated between the use of shared and central resources, and exclusive and local compute power. As of today, available massive distributed deployments of sensors and intelligent devices known as the internet of things (IoT) are confronted with the currently dominating cloud computing model emphasizing centralized shared resources. This model challenges the increasing use of mobile applications and use cases utilizing local resources and information gained from them.

Edge computing is a distributed open platform at the network edge, close to the things or data sources, integrating the capabilities of networks, storage, and applications. By delivering edge intelligence services, edge computing meets the key requirements of industry digitalization for agile connectivity, real-time services, data optimization, application intelligence, security and privacy protection.

Serving as a bridge between the physical and digital worlds, edge computing enables smart assets, smart gateways, smart systems, and smart services.

Edge computing is a method of optimizing cloud computing systems by performing data processing at the edge of the network, near the source of the data.

We can define edge computing as a distributed IT architecture that makes it possible to process data on the periphery – as close to the originating source as possible. If all this sounds gibberish, hold on.

The past decade has seen tremendous growth in the number of internet-connected devices, which has given rise to a technology known as the Internet of Things (IoT). Simply put, IoT is just a concept of inter-connecting various devices and connecting each of the devices to the internet with a simple on/off switch. This includes everything from cell phones, coffee makers, fridge, washing machines, wearable devices, and any device you can think of that easily connects to any device and transfers data seamlessly. As IoT started gaining momentum, a problem arose – that of dealing with the data from these inter-connected devices. There's no need to remind that the data we're talking about is terabytes in size. Traditionally, the data collected from these devices was sent to the organisation's central cloud for processing. However, it was a rather time taking process, owing to the size of the data files. Transferring such large datasets over the network to a central cloud can also expose sensitive organisational data to vulnerabilities.

Edge computing came into the picture to tackle all this and more. Now, have a look at the first para again and allow us to walk you through the definition slowly.

The name 'edge computing' refers to computation around the corner/edge in a network diagram. Edge computing pushes all the significant computational processing power towards the edges of the mesh. Like we said earlier – as close to the originating device as possible.

How does this help?

Consider a smart traffic light. Instead of calling home whenever in need of data analysis, if the device is capable of performing analytics in-house, it can accomplish real-time analysis of streaming data and even communicate with other devices to finish tasks on the go. Edge computing, therefore, speeds up the entire analysis process, enabling quick decision-making.

Edge computing is also beneficial for the organisations as it helps them cut down costs that were earlier incurred on transferring data sets over a network. Other than that, it also allows the organisations to filter out the useful data from the device's periphery itself – thereby enabling organisations to collect only valuable data and ensuring them to cut down costs on cloud computing and storage. Further, edge computing also reduces the response time to milliseconds, all the while conserving the network resources. Using edge computing, we don't necessarily need to send the data over a network. Instead, the local edge computing system is responsible for compiling the data and sending frequent reports to the central cloud storage for long-term storage. Clearly, by only sending the essential data, edge computing drastically reduces the data that traverses the network.

The deployment of Edge Computing is ideal in a variety of situations. One such case is when the IoT devices have weak internet connectivity, and it's not practical for them to be connected to a central cloud constantly.

Other such situation can be when there's a requirement of latency-sensitive processing of data. Edge computing eliminates the factor of latency as the data does not need to be transferred over a network to central cloud storage for processing. This is ideal for financial or manufacturing services where latencies of milliseconds are challenging to achieve.

Why the Edge

Transmitting massive amounts of data is expensive and taxing on network resources. Edge computing allows you to process data near the source and only send relevant data over the network to an intermediate data processor.

For example, a smart refrigerator does not need to continually send internal temperature data back to a cloud analytics dashboard. Rather, it can be configured to only send data when the temperature has changed beyond a particular point; or, it could be polled to send data only when the dashboard is loaded. Similarly, an IoT security camera could only need to send data back to your device when it detects motion or when you explicitly toggle a live data feed.

Edge intelligence is born

The concept of edge intelligence (EI) introduces a paradigm shift with regard to acquiring, storing, and processing data: the data processing is placed at the edge between the data source (e.g. a sensor) and the IoT core and storage services located in the cloud. As such, the literal definition of edge and intelligence specified in Figure 1-1 is adopted: the ability to acquire and apply knowledge and skills is shifted towards the outside of an area, here, the core communication network or the cloud.

EI allows bringing data (pre-)processing and decision-making closer to the data source, which reduces delays in communication. In addition, such (pre-)processing makes it possible to accumulate and condense data before forwarding it to IoT core services in the cloud or storing it, which perfectly matches the capacities offered by the upcoming fifth generation wireless technology (5G) networks providing localized throughput and delay enhancements.

Edge and Realtime

Sensors and remotely deployed devices demand realtime processing. A centralized cloud system is often too slow for this, especially when decisions need to be made in microseconds. This is especially true for IoT devices in regions or locations with poor connectivity.

However, sometimes realtime capabilities demand cloud processing. For example, lets say data consumed by remote tornado weather monitors needs to be sent in realtime to massive supercomputers.

This is where realtime infrastructure comes into play to help enable those data transactions.

Network edge

For internet devices, the network edge is where the device, or the local network containing the device, communicates with the Internet. The edge is a bit of a fuzzy term; for example a user's computer or the processor inside of an IoT camera can be considered the network edge, but the user's router, ISP, or local edge server are also considered the edge. The important takeaway is that the edge of the network is geographically close to the device, unlike origin servers and cloud servers, which can be very far from the devices they communicate with.

Basic Characteristics and Attributes

• Connectivity

Connectivity is the basis of edge computing. The diversity of connected physical objects and application scenarios requires that edge computing provide abundant connection functions such as various network interfaces, protocols, topologies, network deployment and configuration, and network management and maintenance. Connectivity needs to fully draw on the advanced research achievements in the network field, such as TSN, SDN, NFV, NaaS, WLAN, NB-IoT, and 5G. Additionally, connectivity needs to consider interoperability with a variety of existing industrial buses.

• First Entry of Data

As a bridge between the physical and digital worlds, edge computing is the first entry of data. With mass, real-time, and complete data, edge computing implements data management and creates values based on the data E2E lifecycle, supporting innovative applications such as predictive maintenance, asset efficiency and management. In addition, as the first entry of data, edge computing also faces the challenges caused by real-time, determinacy, and diversity.

- Constraint

Edge computing products need to adapt to harsh working conditions and operating environments at industrial sites, such as anti-electromagnetic interference, anti-dust, anti-explosion, anti-vibration, and anti-current/voltage fluctuations. Moreover, in industrial interconnection scenarios, high requirements are imposed on the power consumption, cost, and space of edge computing devices.
Edge computing products need to be integrated and optimized through hardware and software to adapt to various conditions and constraints and support diverse scenarios of industry digitalization.

- Distribution

In actual deployment, edge computing needs to support distributed computing and storage, achieve dynamic scheduling and unified management of distributed resources, support distributed intelligence, and deliver distributed security capabilities.

- Convergence

Convergence of the Operational Technology (OT) and Information and Communications Technology (ICT) is an important foundation for the digital transformation of industries. As the key carrier of "OICT" convergence and collaboration, edge computing must support collaboration in connection, data, management, control, application, and security.

Edge Computing Benefits

Edge computing allows for the clear scoping of computing resources for optimal processing.

- Time-sensitive data can be processed at the point of origin by a localized processor (a device that has its own computing ability).

- Intermediary servers can be used to process data in close geographical proximity to the source (this assumes that intermediate latency is okay, though realtime decisions should be made as close to the origin as possible).

- Cloud servers can be used to process less time sensitive data or to store data for the longterm. With IoT, you'll see this manifest in analytics dashboards.
- Edge application services significantly decrease the volumes of data that must be moved, the consequent traffic, and the distance the data must travel, thereby reducing transmission costs, shrinking latency, and improving quality of service(QoS) (source).

- Edge computing removes a major bottleneck and potential point of failure by de-emphasizing the dependency on the core computing environment.

- Security improves as encrypted data is checked as it passes through protected firewalls and other security points, where viruses, compromised data, and active hackers can be caught early on (source).
- The edge augments scalability by logically grouping CPU capabilities as needed, saving costs on realtime data transmission.

"CROSS" Value of Edge Computing

• Mass and Heterogeneous Connection

Networks are the cornerstone of system interconnection and data aggregation transmission. With the surge in the number of connected devices, networks face enormous challenges in terms of Operations and Maintenance (O&M), management, flexible expansion, and reliability. In addition, a large number of heterogeneous bus connections have long existed at industrial sites, and multi-standard industrial Ethernet coexists. It is a tough issue that must be solved to achieve compatibility among multiple connections and ensure real-time reliability of connections.

• Real-Time Services

Industrial system testing, control, and implementation have high real-time requirements, even within 10 milliseconds in some scenarios. If data analysis and control logic are implemented only on the cloud, it is difficult to meet the real-time requirements of services.

• Data Optimization

Today, industrial sites contain a large amount of heterogeneous data. Data optimization must be implemented for data aggregation and unified presentation and openness, so that the data can serve intelligent edge applications in a flexible and efficient manner.

• Smart Applications
Business process optimization, O&M automation, and service innovation drive applications to be smart. Edge intelligence delivers significant efficiency and cost advantages. Intelligent applications represented by predictive maintenance are driving industries to transition to new service models and business models.

• Security and Privacy Protection
Security is critical to cloud and edge computing, requiring end-to-end protection. The network edge is close to Internet of Things (IoT) devices, making access control and threat protection difficult. Edge security includes device security, network security, data security, and application security. The integrity and confidentiality of key data, as well as protection of mass production or personal data are also key areas of focus for security.

Figure 1.1: Edge & Cloudlets

Cloud computing is suitable for non-real-time, long-period data and business decision-making scenarios, while edge computing plays an irreplaceable role in scenarios such as real-time, short-period data and local decision-making.

Edge and cloud computing are two important foundations for the digital transformation of industries. The collaboration between them in respect of network, service, application, and intelligence will help support more scenarios and unleash greater value in industry digitalization.

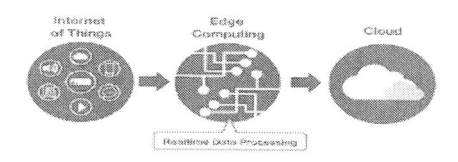

Figure 1.2: 1 Points of collaboration between edge computing and cloud computing

Point of Collaboration	Edge Computing	Cloud Computing
Network	Data aggregation (TSN + OPCUA)	Data analysis

Service	Agent	Service orchestration
Application	Micro applications	Lifecycle management of applications
Intelligence	Distributed reasoning	Centralized training

Edge Computing Scenario

Volume versus available bandwidth

Devices and sensors can produce more data than is economically feasible to transmit to the cloud. To address this problem, analytical algorithms can be applied at the edge to process the incoming sensor data and only send higher level events to the core.

For example, tens or hundreds of cameras produce video streams at 60 frames per second. Even with compression, the transmission of video streams can be very costly. A video analysis service could be deployed at the edge that identifies people, objects (e.g. vehicles), and their properties (e.g. license plates and x,y coordinates). Only this higher level information would then be sent to the core.

The video content would be stored locally at the edge for a certain duration and could be accessed by a human operator for further analysis as needed.

IoT solutions are often cost sensitive, and communication costs specifically represent a significant portion of ongoing expenses. Low bandwidth wide area protocol solutions such as LoRA, Sigfox and others, can reduce the communication cost. But these solutions come with the unwanted consequences associated with low bandwidth, such as reduced performance.

Thus, communication costs can be addressed more effectively by using analytical algorithms to process the incoming sensor data and only send alerts (another form of higher level events) to the core. This also enables confidential or privacy related data to be kept near the data source so that the disclosure of data can be limited.

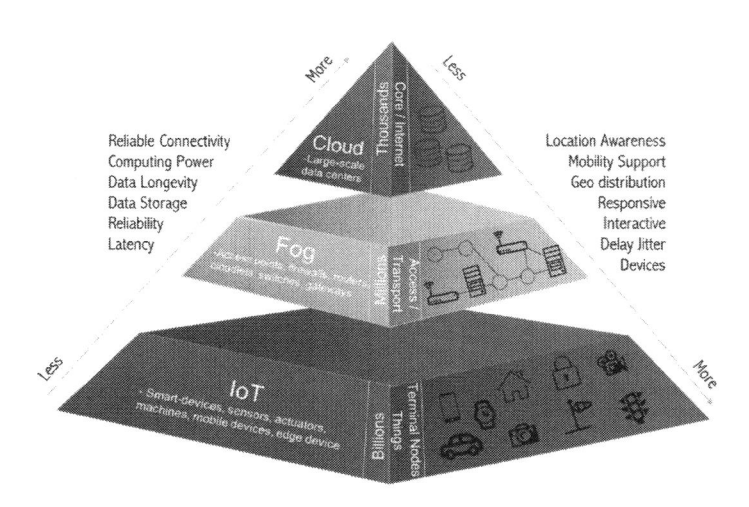

Figure 1.3: Edge Scenario

Comparing Fog Computing with Edge Computing

With the proliferation of mobile and connected devices, massive volume velocity of data is being generated with high velocity. According to Gartner, *there will be more than 20.4 billion connected devices all over the world by 2020.*
As the data explodes, cloud wouldn't be enough to handle the flood of information, devices, and interactions. Cloud computing allows easier access to compute, for storage and connectivity. However, it works as a centralized resource which can result in delays to act on data.

When an internet of things (IoT) device generates data, it is sent back for processing to a centralized cloud or data centre source. But by the time this data is processed, the chance to act on it might no longer exist.

For example, if the temperature of a chemical tank is about to cross its acceptable limit, the action will need to be taken within seconds. A connected device will send the data to the cloud for analysis, and by the time everything gets done, there will be no opportunity to prevent a spoiled batch.

Edge computing and fog computing are the technologies that can address this problem. These technologies push capabilities of processing and intelligence at the source of data generation, rather than sending it to the cloud or data centre. The main difference between edge computing and fog computing is exactly where the processing power and intelligence are pushed.

Edge computing

14

Computing which happens close to the source of data generation, rather than depending on a centralized cloud for data processing, is called edge computing.

Edge computing (also known as edge) eliminates the time and distance required to send data to the cloud. It doesn't mean that there is no need for cloud. It means that the cloud comes to the device. This enhances speed and performance for transporting the data, along with devices and applications on the edge.

Edge computing has the potential to enable dynamic communication among several things. Imagine a driverless car sending data for processing to the cloud, which may take a long time to analyse data. This may result in accidents. Edge computing seeks to accommodate that. It will process data in real-time at the car itself.

The global edge computing market will reach $3.24 billion by 2025, according to a recent report by Million Insights.

Fog computing

Fog computing involves bringing intelligence to local area network architecture and processing the data in a fog node.
Concept of fog computing was given by Cisco in 2014. According to Cisco, *fog computing is a standard that defines the way edge computing should work, and it enables the operation of compute, storage and networking services between end devices and cloud computing data centres.*
What this means is that it works as a layer to define the location of data generation and the location of that data to be stored, like cloud or customer's data centre.

Edge computing vs fog computing

Data generated from IoT devices can be processed at three locations: cloud, network, or device itself. As mentioned above, if data is processed in the cloud, it will take a lot of time to get analysed. So, it is better to process it either on the network or in the device.

Both the technologies bring intelligence and data to analytics platforms located close to the source of data generation, like speakers, motors, screens, sensors, etc. The aim of these technologies is to reduce latency issues, while depending on the cloud to analyse data and make quicker data-driven decisions.

So, what is the difference between edge computing and fog computing?

The key difference between fog computing and edge computing is associated with the location where the data is processed.

In edge computing, the data is processed right on the devices, or gateway devices closest to the sensors. So, the compute and storage systems are located at the edge, close to device, application, or component producing the data.

Whereas, in fog computing, edge computing processing is moved to processors linked to a local area network or into the hardware of LAN. Therefore, the data in fog computing is processed within an IoT gateway or fog node in LAN.

Long story short: Edge computing places the intelligence in the connected devices themselves, whereas, fog computing puts it in the local area network.

Advantages of edge computing and fog computing

- Real-time data analysis: Since the data is processed at the source of data generation, it can be analysed in real-time or near real-time.
- Reduced costs: These technologies lower the costs as companies need less data bandwidth management solutions for local devices, as compared to the cloud or data centre.
- Lower bandwidth consumption: Companies wouldn't need high bandwidth to handle data, because processing will happen at the edge itself.
- Lower latency levels: This is the main benefit of edge computing and fog computing. They lower the latency compared to a faraway cloud or data centre by eliminating the time involved in sending data back and forth.

Applications of edge computing

- #### Oil and gas industry
Edge computing holds a key role in the oil and gas industry. Several IoT devices are deployed to monitor temperature, humidity, pressure, moisture and many other factors. The data generated from these devices provides insights about the health of the systems.

Analysing and processing the data in real-time helps the industry to prevent several incidents.

- #### Intelligent transportation and traffic management
IoT technology is being used to effectively manage traffic and transportation. Since the traffic data is gathered using sensors and cameras, it needs to be acted upon in real-time, otherwise it will be of no use. Edge computing processes massive amounts of data on the traffic hardware itself, while reducing operational and storage costs.

- #### Self-driving vehicles
Although self-driving vehicles have not become the norm, edge computing is a necessary technology for them. It will be impossible for such vehicles to work without analysing data in real-time.

Driverless vehicles host artificial intelligence and IoT applications at the edge, so that latency levels between data generated and used to run vehicles is extremely low.

Applications of fog computing

- ### Smart cities
There are a lot of challenges for large cities like public safety, traffic congestion, high energy usage, municipal services, etc. Fog computing can help in addressing these challenges by deploying a network of fog nodes, forming a single IoT network.

Many cities are failing to transform into smart ones, because of broadband bandwidth and connectivity issues. Deployment of fog nodes can optimize the bandwidth, while providing local storage and processing.

- ### Smart buildings
To make large buildings smarter, thousands of sensors will be needed for measuring several parameters like keycard readers, temperature, occupancy of parking space, etc. Fog computing can be implemented in such buildings for autonomous operations.

The smart buildings will have fog nodes on each floor to monitor the functions, control lights and other electric appliances, etc. It will also provide compute and storage infrastructure to complement capabilities of mobile devices.

For example, a sensor will generate data when it senses smoke, and then process it to fog nodes in real-time for further actions.

- ### Visual security
For security purposes, cameras are installed everywhere in public places like parking lots, shopping malls, restaurants, etc. The data from these cameras require high storage and bandwidth to carry it to the cloud. Also, it can't be analysed in real-time.

By implementing a fog computing architecture, the video processing for sensitive surveillance systems can be divided between fog nodes. This can enable real-time tracking and detection of anomalies or any other such activities.

Companies working on fog computing development

The leading companies from the cloud industry who had a collective vision that fog computing can transform IoT and other digital concepts, founded a joint ecosystem for it. Called OpenFog Consortium, the ecosystem was founded in 2015 by Arm Holdings, Cisco, Dell, Intel, Microsoft, and Princeton University

Since then, many large organizations, startups, research institutions and universities have joined the OpenFog Consortium. The contributing members of the OpenFog include Foxconn, Hitachi, Sakura Internet, Shanghai Tech University, etc.

COMPATABILITY OF CLOUD, FOG AND EDGE COMPUTING

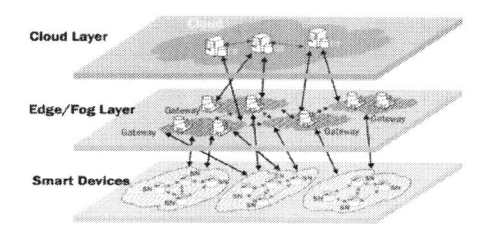

Figure1.4: Compatibility of Cloud, Fog and Edge

Organizations that rely heavily on data are increasingly likely to use cloud, fog, and edge computing infrastructures. These architectures allow organizations to take advantage of a variety of computing and data storage resources, including the Industrial Internet of Things (IIoT). Cloud, fog and edge computing may appear similar, but they are different layers of the IIoT. Edge computing for the IIoT allows processing to be performed locally at multiple decision points for the purpose of reducing network traffic. Industrial embedded computer systems can leverage the power of the IIoT to enable the successful design of high-performing industrial applications.

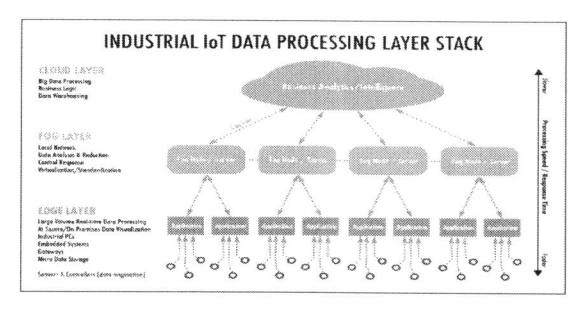

Figure 1.5: Layer Stack

Cloud Computing

Most enterprises areu familiar with cloud computing since it's now a de facto standard in many industries. Fog and edge computing are both extensions of cloud networks, which are a collection of servers comprising a distributed network. Such a network can allow an organization to greatly exceed the resources that would otherwise be available to it, freeing organizations from the requirement to keep infrastructure on site. The primary advantage of cloud-based systems is they allow data to be collected from multiple sites and devices, which is accessible anywhere in the world.

Embedded hardware obtains data from on-site IIoT devices and passes it to the fog layer. Pertinent data is then passed to the cloud layer, which is typically in a different geographical location. The cloud layer is thus able to benefit from IIoT devices by receiving their data through the other layers. Organizations often achieve superior results by integrating a cloud platform with on-site fog networks or edge devices. Most enterprises are now migrating towards a fog or edge infrastructure to increase the utilization of their end-user and IIoT devices.

The use of embedded systems and other specialized devices allows these organizations to better leverage the processing capability available to them, resulting in improved network performance. The increased distribution of data processing and storage made possible by these systems reduces network traffic, thus improving operational efficiency. The cloud also performs high-order computations such as predictive analysis and business control, which involves the processing of large amounts of data from multiple sources. These computations are then passed back down the computation stack so that it can be used by human operators and to facilitate machine-to-machine (M2M) communications and machine learning.

Fog Computing

Fog computing and edge computing appear similar since they both involve bringing intelligence and processing closer to the creation of data. However, the key difference between the two lies in where the location of intelligence and compute power is placed. A fog environment places intelligence at the local area network (LAN). This architecture transmits data from endpoints to a gateway, where it is then transmitted to sources for processing and return transmission. Edge computing places intelligence and processing power in devices such as embedded automation controllers.

For example, a jet engine test produces a large amount of data about the engine's performance and condition very quickly. Industrial gateways are often used in this application to collect data from edge devices, which is then sent to the LAN for processing.

Fog computing uses edge devices and gateways with the LAN providing processing capability. These devices need to be efficient, meaning they require little power and produce little heat. Single-board computers (SBCs) can be used in a fog environment to receive real-time data such as response time (latency), security and data volume, which can be distributed across multiple nodes in a network.

Edge Computing

The IoT has introduced a virtually infinite number of endpoints to commercial networks. This trend has made it more challenging to consolidate data and processing in a single data center, giving rise to the use of "edge computing." This architecture performs computations near the edge of the network, which is closer to the data source.

Edge computing is an extension of older technologies such as peer-to-peer networking, distributed data, self-healing network technology and remote cloud services. It's powered by small form factor hardware with flash-storage arrays that provide highly optimized performance. The processors used in edge computing devices offer improved hardware security with a low power requirement. Industrial embedded SBCs and data acquisition modules provide gateways for the data flow to and from an organization's computing environments.

The IIoT is composed of edge, fog and cloud architectural layers, such that the edge and fog layers complement each other. Fog computing uses a centralized system that interacts with industrial gateways and embedded computer systems on a local area network, whereas edge computing performs much of the processing on embedded computing platforms directly interfacing to sensors and controllers. However, this distinction isn't always clear, since organizations can be highly variable in their approach to data processing.

Edge computing offers many advantages over traditional architectures such as optimizing resource usage in a cloud-computing system. Performing computations at the edge of the network reduces network traffic, which reduces the risk of a data bottleneck. Edge computing also improves security by encrypting data closer to the network core, while optimizing data that's further from the core for performance. Control is very important for edge computing in industrial environments because it requires a bidirectional process for handling data. Embedded systems can collect data at a network's edge in real time and process that data before handing it off to the higher-level computing environments.

Use cases of Edge Computing

Drones are capable of reaching remote places that human can't even think of. Edge computing enables these drones to review, analyze, and respond to the analysis in real-time. For instance, if a drone finds any emergency situation, it can instantaneously provide valuable information to people nearby without having first to send the data over a network and then receive the analysis.

Augmented Reality– The introduction of edge computing has taken Augmented Reality a step further. An edge computing platform can provide highly localised data targeted at user's point of interest; thereby enhancing the AR services.

Automated vehicles– Giants like Google and Uber are coming up with self-driving cars. Edge computing plays a crucial role in the development of such automatic vehicles. These vehicles can process and transmit vital data in real-time to other vehicles commuting nearby using edge computing. These giants aim to make such self-driving cars a consumer reality by 2020. With the introduction of such automated vehicles, we're sure to see a decrease in the number of lives lost due to automobile accidents.
Having said all this, there are still some compromises and challenges that can't be neglected when talking about edge computing. First of all, only a minute subset of the whole data is processed and analyzed on edge. Then, the analysis of this data is transmitted over the network.

This means that we are ideally disregarding some of the raw, unanalyzed data, and potentially missing out on some insights. Again, an important question arises – how bearable is this "loss" of data? Does the organisation need the whole data or is the result generated enough for them? Will missing out on some data negatively affect the organisation's analysis?

There's no correct answer to these questions. An aeroplane system can't afford to miss any data, even a bit of it (no pun intended), so, all of the data should be transferred and analyzed to detect trends and patterns. But, transferring data during flight time is not a good idea. So, a better approach will be to collect the data offline and perform edge computing during the flight time. All in all, edge computing is not a panacea in the world of Information Technology. It is a relatively newer technology that offers a host of benefits. However, it's still important to know if it fits your organisation's needs or not. The bottom line is that data is valuable. All data that can be analyzed should be analyzed to detect patterns and gain insights. In today's world, data-driven companies are making a lot more progress compared to the traditional ones. Edge Analytics is a new and exciting space and is an answer for maintenance and usability of data, and we can expect to see many more exciting applications of the same in the years to come.

Drawbacks of Edge Computing

One drawback of edge computing is that it can increase attack vectors. With the addition of more 'smart' devices into the mix, such as edge servers and IoT devices that have robust built-in computers, there are new opportunities for malicious actors to compromise these devices.

Another drawback with edge computing is that it requires more local hardware. For example, while an IoT camera needs a built-in computer to send its raw video data to a web server, it would require a much more sophisticated computer with more processing power in order for it to run its own motion-detection algorithms. But the dropping costs of hardware are making it cheaper to build smarter devices.

Edge computing terms and definitions

Like most technology areas, edge computing has its own lexicon. Here are brief definitions of some of the more commonly used terms

- Edge devices: These can be any device that produces data. These could be sensors, industrial machines or other devices that produce or collect data.

- Edge: What the edge is depends on the use case. In a telecommunications field, perhaps the edge is a cell phone or maybe it's a cell tower. In an automotive scenario, the edge of the network could be a car. In manufacturing, it could be a machine on a shop floor; in enterprise IT, the edge could be a laptop.

- Edge gateway: A gateway is the buffer between where edge computing processing is done and the broader fog network. The gateway is the window into the larger environment beyond the edge of the network.

- Fat client: Software that can do some data processing in edge devices. This is opposed to a thin client, which would merely transfer data.

- Edge computing equipment: Edge computing uses a range of existing and new equipment. Many devices, sensors and machines can be outfitted to work in an edge computing environment by simply making them Internet-accessible. Cisco and other hardware vendors have a line of ruggedized network equipment that has hardened exteriors meant to be used in field environments. A range of compute servers, converged systems and even storage-based hardware systems like Amazon Web Service's Snowball can be used in edge computing deployments.

- Mobile edge computing: This refers to the buildout of edge computing systems in telecommunications systems, particularly 5G scenarios.

Chapter 2.
The evolution of computing models towards edge computing

Shared and central resources versus exclusive and local computation

The computing models of the last seven decades are now oscillating between the use of shared and central resources or exclusive and local compute power. Key factors in deciding the direction of the curve are advances in computing and communication. Cheap and powerful compute power pushes towards the use of local resources. Cheap and fast communication technologies enable the use of shared, central resources.

Models which relied heavily on shared resources included mainframes operated in batch mode or which were controlled by text-only terminals. At the opposite end of the spectrum, the standalone personal computers (PCs) of the 1980s were powered by affordable compute power.

Networked PCs and client-server models created a more balanced computing model between the two extremes enabled by high-speed local area networks.

The pendulum swung back towards central resources with the early web model enabled by cheap and fast wide area networking, compared to the level of data being transferred.

Today's dominating cloud computing model still emphasizes centralized shared resources, but mobile apps and JavaScript-heavy web applications often make good use of local resources.

Shared and centralized resources are highly efficient, as they maximize the utilization of compute resources and provide elasticity. Given their central location, typically in data centres, they can be more easily secured, and their lifecycle management is less complex than in distributed systems. However, they need highly available communication channels of sufficient bandwidth and speed to reach end users, which may incur significant cost.

Exclusive and local resources can work in isolation, but the compute power, memory and storage are limited and may be insufficient for certain tasks.

As such devices are often under end user control, securing and managing them, as well as the lifecycle of their applications, becomes more complex.

The cloud computing model seems to have found a happy compromise in the distributed computing spectrum, balancing the pros and cons between exclusive/local versus shared/central, but this solution will not last.

IoT disrupts the cloud

The IoT disrupts the cloud compute model by introducing new usage scenarios resulting in the following key requirements:

• Real-time: Often, decisions need to be made within tens of milliseconds. Today's communication infrastructure and the laws of physics require local decision-making, as a roundtrip to the cloud would take an excessive amount of time.

• Connectivity: Today's mobile networks are often spotty and cannot guarantee connectivity to the cloud. Hence, decision-making must occur locally.

• Data volume: The amount of data generated by sensors can be huge; for example, hundreds of high-resolution cameras creating video streams at 30 frames per second, which could clog wide-area communication channels.

• Context: The business context needed for interpreting IoT data for decision-making is typically held in centralized enterprise systems.

The disruption of the cloud model is not the displacement of the cloud but rather its extension to the edge.

Characteristics of the new computing model

The cloud will continue to exist. For example, certain functions are best performed in the cloud, such as the training of predictive analytics algorithms, as typically only the cloud holds the necessary data in its entirety.

Devices will have compute and storage capabilities; for instance, high-end security cameras can store and analyse videos on the device.

Edge computing will provide compute power and storage in the space between the device and the cloud. Edge compute devices include IoT gateways, routers, and micro data centres in mobile network base stations, on the shop floor and in vehicles, among other places.

The new model will be a fully distributed computing model. It will support a wide range of interaction and communication paradigms, including the following:

• Autonomous, local decision-making based on incoming IoT data and cached enterprise information

• Peer-to-peer networking, for example, security cameras communicating amongst themselves about an object within their scope

• Edge networking, for example, platoon driving, i.e. vehicles self-organizing into groups which travel together, orchestrated and controlled by a micro data centre in the base station of a mobile network

• Distributed queries across data that is stored in devices, in the cloud and anywhere in between

• Distributed data management, for example, data aging: which data to store, where and for how long

• Self-learning algorithms that learn and execute on the edge, or learn in the cloud and execute on the edge, or learn and execute in the cloud

- Isolation, involving devices which are disconnected for a long time, operating on minimal energy consumption to maximize lifespan

Through the introduction of intelligence at the edge nodes, systems can:

- take decisions more quickly and efficiently, as the roundtrip delay in contacting the cloud is removed;

- reach decisions according to local identity management and access control policies, securing the data close to its source;

- reduce communication costs by limiting communication over public wide area networks.

The opportunities come from technology evolutions in manufactured devices and 5G networks, along with concepts, algorithms and Standards in software-defined networking, mobile edge computing, analytics and device and data ownership.

Blueprint of edge computing intelligence

Definition and high level architecture

This defines EI as the infrastructure nodes that span from devices, corporate networks and public or dedicated networks up to the cloud deployments of the service.
This means that several IT and OT technologies can be placed so close to the edge of the network that aspects such as real-time networks, security capabilities to ensure cybersecurity, self-learning solutions and personalized/customized connectivity can be addressed. This radical transformation from the cloud to the edge will support trillions of sensors and billions of systems and will treat data in motion differently from data at rest.

Application areas

IoT
From a network architecture perspective, the core of such an IoT solution is typically a central IT system, bearing the name of IoT core server, in charge of storing, processing and analysing IoT data (see Figure 2-2). Much of this IoT data often can be located in the cloud, away from the core.

IoT endpoints (i.e. devices with sensors and/or actuators) frequently do not have the communication capabilities to transmit all their sensor data in a secure, reliable and cost-efficient manner to the core. The most common obstacles to such transmission include the following:

- Sensors may only support low energy protocols to conserve battery power.

- Mobile devices leveraging cellular communication lack coverage in certain locations.

- Mobile communication links are often bandwidth-constrained or expensive.

- Wide area connections can introduce too much latency for real-time decision-making.

Furthermore, certain local systems, for example, self-driving vehicles, must autonomously make decisions in real-time and cannot wait for instructions sent from the cloud.

EI can address these challenges. An IoT gateway is an example of an ECN. It connects to devices that are located away from the core (often referred to as 'devices at the edge') via communication protocols such as low-energy Bluetooth or ZigBee. At the same time, it also connects to the core directly using high-speed internet. Additionally, gateways provide security and lifecycle management at the edge, such that the edge is a sustainable and manageable compute unit. The hardware used for such gateways ranges from high-powered, rack-mounted servers to smaller devices with embedded processors, and anything in between.

IoT edge computing refers to the capability of processing, storing, and analysing sensor data as well as performing decision-making at ECNs.

The role of the ECN is:

1. To retrieve or pull IoT data from endpoints and content of a varied nature (e.g. media, enterprise bound, maps) from the IoT core servers, in order to be able to undertake data and networking analytics, take decisions on current information and self-adapt the local knowledge;

2. Based on the decision taken, to trigger an action towards the endpoints (e.g. actuate or change the threshold) or even send notifications towards the IoT core servers, e.g. request resources in terms of core computing, networking quality of service or dispatch of rescue forces, in case of fire or other dangerous situations.

Analysts, for example, the International Data Corporation (IDC), indicate that 40% of IoT-created data will be subject to IoT edge computing, and that this ratio of edge-to-core data and processing is growing annually [3].

Content delivery networks

A content delivery network (CDN) is a distributed network of servers bringing content to end users. The goal of a CDN is to optimize content delivery with high availability and performance, while minimizing required bandwidth in the backbone and saving transportation costs. Instead of using a centralized server at a single location, content is delivered from servers situated near the endpoints. With CDNs, the traditional client-server model is split into two communication flows: one between end user and proxy media server and the other from the media server to the central server.

The advantages of CDNs include reduction of latency, limiting the impact of server and network failures and minimizing wide area transportation costs. A CDN also strengthens security. By being highly distributed, it can absorb the effects of less-sophisticated malicious attacks. The deployment of a CDN plays an essential role in the business strategy of content providers, leading to an improvement in the quality of experience of the customers. Enhancing user satisfaction represents a key factor for high conversion rates in online business, i.e. the number of website visitors actually performing desired actions such as purchase, subscription or ad-clicks.

CDN technology especially supports the delivery of large media files and streaming content, but other sites with heavy traffic that serve a large widely geographically distributed user community, e.g. social media or e-commerce in general, also benefit from CDNs.

Today CDNs serve a large fraction of the internet content. Such content may consist of web objects (text, graphics and scripts), downloadable objects (media files, software, documents), applications (e-commerce, portals), traffic from social networks and especially on-demand streaming media and live streaming media. A number of major companies specialize in the provisioning of CDN services, but support of CDN has also become part of the portfolio of global cloud services providers, internet service providers (ISPs) and network operators.

CDNs are derived from technologies for website acceleration, including server farms and intelligent caching. The CDN market started to develop in the late 1990s triggered by higher demand for audio and video streaming and growing volumes of content. With the further development of the technologies, additional factors such as cloud computing, energy awareness and user demand for more interactivity came into focus. Flash crowd phenomena observed in the context of events such as the 9/11 terrorist attacks created awareness concerning the importance of CDN solutions. The need for CDN services generated initiatives aimed at developing Standards for delivering broadband content and streaming rich media content (video, audio and associated data) over the internet.

The recent evolution of CDNs has been strongly driven by the continuing trend toward mobile end devices combined with a user expectation of receiving performance at least equal to conventional fixed or stationary devices. For creating a personalized interactive user experience, dynamic content generation needs to be supported with individually created suggestions and offers, without compromising download times and page rendering. As CDNs become increasingly sophisticated, the integration of multiple CDNs from different providers is often required.

CDNs form a major use case for increased EI. Media content is becoming even more localized, real-time and bandwidth-intensive. Hence, more intelligence at the edge is needed to address these challenges.

Tactile internet

The capability to transmit touch in perceived real-time, which is enabled by suitable robotics and haptics equipment at the edges together with an unprecedented communications network, is often referred to as the "tactile internet" [4]. Thus, tactile internet stands for near real-time human-machine interaction, including cases in which the human is mobile. The use cases and opportunities enabled by the tactile internet are numerous and the performance requirements of networks are highly demanding.

The latency requirements for the tactile internet are very challenging, with a round trip delay of 1 ms or less typically required. 4G mobile networks can offer about a 25 ms latency under ideal conditions, which is way off the 1 ms mark required. 5G promises to deliver ultra-low latency for a number of critical use cases, including industry automation, robotics, remote surgery, etc. Such latency can only be achieved by deploying new hardware in the air interface as well as through deployment of edge clouds. Furthermore, such latency requirements dictate the maximum distance from the sensor to the mobile edge cloud, restricted by the speed of light.

The use of edge clouds is necessary to fulfil the latency requirements of the tactile internet. However, edge clouds are also required in order to provide storage and computation for tactile internet services. Scalability, security and reliability are highlighted as critical characteristics of such edge computing in order to serve use cases such as remote surgery and industry automation, which are described below. The deployment options of edge real-time feedback is imperative to ensure clouds which determine a number of factors, including that a process or endpoint is operating scalability and latency by correctly deploying small cloudlets. Currently such systems are hard or very close to radio base stations which can be wired, for example, industrial Ethernet.

Implementation and Expectations from this Technology

Many organizations have begun to implement edge computing in their IoT environment because it saves a lot of time taken by the devices to communicate with their host in order to take the necessary decisions. Edge computing processes the data instantly where it is created which provides instant results and decisions. This benefits organizations in many ways like cost savings, less time taken to interact with a cloud, instant analysis, and faster responses to clients.

There is a huge amount of data being generated every day through computer-to-computer communications and IoT devices which eventually comes down to processing this data. For example, let's assume there are multiple devices installed in a city which creates and transmits massive measures of information. It is a big investment which demands data analysis tools to process huge measures of information. These tools offer real-time analysis of the data being collected by various devices and provide reports and results instantly.

There are mainly 4 vital drivers pushing us towards the edge computing:

- Evolving customer expectations from their own business;
- Optimum use of data to explore new possibilities;
- Upcoming technologies in networking and software which offers opportunities in edge computing;
- Application on edge platforms like IoT devices which processes and transforms data through a network for better customer experience and better delivery of data.

Chapter 3.
Mobile-Edge Computing

Mobile cloud computing

In recent years, we are witnessing significant demand from users for different types of cloud services on their mobile devices; for instance, services in entertainment, social networking, business, news, games or health and well being. However, this demand results in mobile devices facing issues like low energy, poor resources and low connectivity. To address this, the term Mobile Cloud Computing (MCC) came to light and researchers try to define the boundaries and give proper definitions.

There are several existing definitions for Mobile Cloud Computing. In general, it is a running service on a resource rich cloud server which is used by a thin mobile client. It can also be referred when mobile nodes play the role of resource provider in a peer-to-peer network. We can take the need for adaptability, scalability, availability and self-awareness in cloud computing concept and expand it to mobile cloud computing.

Mobile cloud computing in its simplest form, refers to an infrastructure where both the data storage and data processing happen outside of the mobile device. Mobile cloud applications move the computing power and data storage away from mobile phones and into the cloud, bringing applications and MCC to not just smartphone users but a much broader range of mobile subscribers.

MCC tackles certain challenges of mobile devices in a desirable manner. Energy efficiency is reached by several solutions like intelligent access to disk or screen. In addition, data storage capacity and processing power are improved through storing and accessing big data on the cloud. Also, we can have more reliability by storing our data on the cloud on different cloud servers.

However, despite all improvements by MCC, there are still issues to be addressed like low bandwidth, high latency, service availability, quality of service (QoS) and service cost. Bandwidth is limited in wireless networks compared to normal wired networks. Users need high availability despite mobile devices' lack of connectivity and they demand better QoS and lower service cost. Moreover, network latency is still a big burden in improving user experience by getting the way of cloud services. These matters are more tangible in applications that virtual reality services which demand low latency and high bandwidth.

Therefore, considering the previously discussed weaknesses, utilizing resources in user proximity and improving the locality of services seems to improve the availability, connectivity and network latency.

Cloudlets

As depicted in Figure 3.1, cloudlet is considered as the middle tier of a 3-tier hierarchy: mobile device, cloudlet and cloud. A cloudlet can also be viewed as a resource rich centre at the proximity of users. Cloudlet is connected to a larger cloud server and its goal is to bring the cloud services closer to the end-user.

In the cloudlet concept, mobile device offloads its workload to a resource-rich, local cloudlet. Cloudlets would be situated in common areas such as coffee shops, libraries or university halls, so that mobile devices can connect and function as a thin client to the cloudlet. A cloudlet could be any first hop element at the edge of network while it has four key attributes. It has only soft state, it should be resource rich and well-connected, with low end-to-end latency and also it follows a certain standard for offloading (e.g. Virtual machine migration). In other words, a cloudlet's failure is

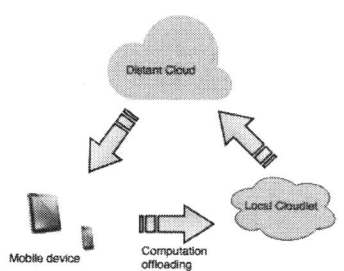

Figure 3.1: Cloudlet's architecture

not critical; it has strong internal connectivity and high bandwidth wireless LAN and it should be in logical and physical proximity of the user to reduce the network latency.

There are two main approaches to implement cloudlet infrastructure using Virtual Machine (VM) technology. In both of these architectures, it is important that cloudlet could go back to its beginning state after being used (e.g. by post-use clean up). A VM based approach is broadly used since it can cleanly encapsulate and separate the transient guest software environment from the cloudlet infrastructure's permanent host software and it's less brittle than other approaches like process migration or software virtualization.

Regarding implementation, it should be possible to transfer a VM state from the user's mobile application to cloudlet's infrastructure. The first approach is VM migration in which an already executing VM is suspended and its state of processor, disk and memory will be transferred to destination and execution will be resumed from exact state of suspension in the cloudlet host environment. The second approach is dynamic VM synthesis which mobile device delivers a small VM overlay - instead of the mentioned states in first approach - to cloudlet infrastructure that possesses the VM base. The overlay is calculated by mobile device based on the customized image encapsulating the requirements of the application. Then the overlay is executed in the exact state that it was suspended and the result will be returned by the cloudlet.

Cloudlets utilize rapidly deployed VMs which the client can customize freely upon their need to make the VM image or VM overlay which has the application and all necessary requirements to run properly. In both types

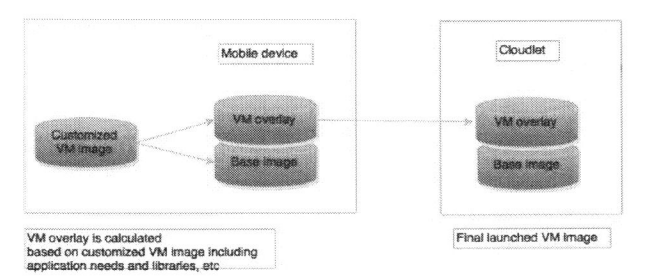

Figure 3.2: Cloudlet dynamic VM synthesis

of implementations, the VM image or overlay is created at runtime by the user which is quite exible for overloading the workload to the cloudlet. Nevertheless, despite this exibility, the procedure of creating an image or a VM overlay and also application status encapsulation could be quite time consuming. At the end, it is totally dependent on application design, needs and environment whether to choose using cloudlets as resource rich sources or not.

Mobile-Edge computing

Yet after all, it is notable that the business model of cloudlets is not clear. In other words, who's going to play the role of network edge? Is it going to be only dedicated to private clouds which have the possibility of deploying cloudlets in their local network? Is there going to be any standards to increase the simplicity and also to encourage developers to create useful applications?

Realizing the advantages of bringing cloud services and resources closer, the cloudlet concept got the attention of Radio Access Network (RAN) operators, as it is a reasonably valid idea to use RAN base stations as the very first hop of network edge to serve mobile users. Hence, serious efforts have begun to make this idea practical for business environment. As an example, recently Nokia Networks introduced their new generation of intelligent base stations which are considered as edge computing platform enabled base stations (known as: **Nokia Radio Application Cloud Server (RACS))**.

Furthermore, ETSI (European Telecommunications Standards Institute) with cooperation of operators such as Huawei, IBM, Intel, Nokia Networks, NTT DOCOMO and Vodafone has formed an Industry Specification Group (ISG) to create a standardized and open environment platform for bringing cloud services closer to the end-users and to formulate a logical integration of mobile applications on such platform between vendors, service providers and third party developers. In other words, the objective is to create an initiative for Mobile-Edge Computing (MEC).

In ETSI's executive briefing, MEC is defined as follows:

"Mobile-edge Computing offers application developers and content providers cloud-computing capabilities and an IT service environment at the edge of the mobile network. This environment is characterized by ultra-low latency and high bandwidth as well as real-time access to radio network information that can be leveraged by applications."

MEC's goal is to transform base stations into high performance customizable intelligent service hubs on the edge of mobile networks while it generates revenue and unique value for operators from offering different value propositions to mobile users, such as proximity of resources, context and location awareness, agility and speed.

A MEC-enabled base-station provides developers with the ability of running an application on the network edge using a predefined standard platform. This platform might also offer some extra services such as cloud storage, caching, computing, etc to the application. Practically, this turns the base-station into a MEC server. A MEC server can be deployed at different types of LTE (Long-Term Evolution) base stations such as ENodeB or 3G RNC (Radio Network Controller). Figure 3.3 illustrates the general architecture of MEC.

To conclude, MEC is a new ecosystem which enables MNOs to provide authorized third parties with a platform to access RAN edge and deploy unique applications based on MEC features. Finally, these advantages enhance quality of experience (QoE) for mobile subscribers and bring value for operators, letting them play complementary and profitable roles within their respective business models.

Nokia Networks Solution to MEC

To keep pace with the trend of evolution in mobile base-stations, Nokia Networks recently announced their new generation of intelligent base-stations.

These base-stations are equipped with Nokia Networks Radio Applications

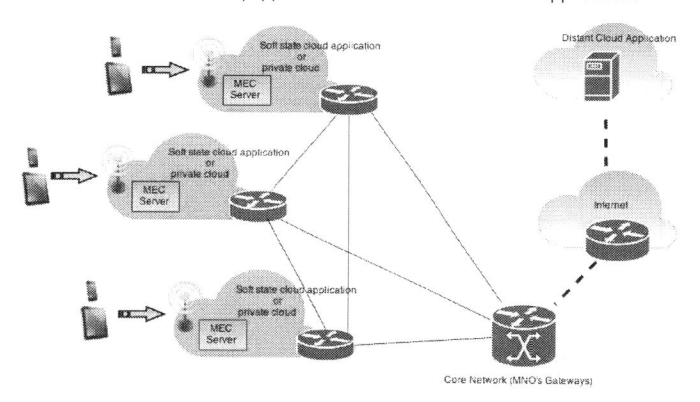

Figure 3.3: Architecture of Mobile-Edge Computing

Cloud Servers (RACS). RACS has both capabilities of a radio base-station and a MEC cloud server. Cloud applications can be developed on the RACS by third party developers and mobile users can get serviced by these applications while they are connected to one RACS.

On the RACS, applications are encapsulated and run in a virtual machine (VM) on the top of Nokia Networks application engine (see Figure 3.4). Each VM is customized according to the requirements of the application. When an application is deployed in Nokia Networks network, it means this customized VM is replicated on all the RACS. Each application with certain type of service is encapsulated in a different VM to keep applications from interfering with each other's services and also to make the run-time environment more secure. In Nokia Networks terminology, these applications are called Liquid Applications.

Regarding developers' point of view, Liquid Apps are distributed system applications and all the principles of distributed systems are valid in the environment. Particularly all the distributed system apps can be utilized and deployed on RACS. Nokia Networks has an application life cycle process for third party developers. This process is called AppFactory. AppFactory consists of verification of the app idea, help and support in the development phase (e.g. test environment and simulation support), validation of developed app, publishing on the Nokia Networks RACS network and at the end,

32

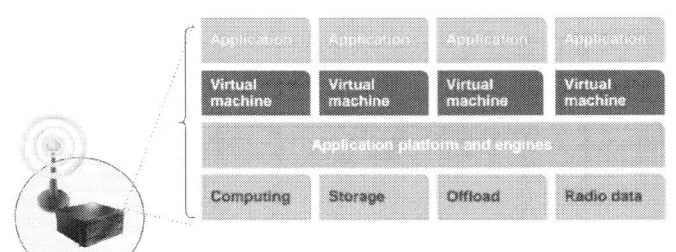

Figure 3.4: Nokia Networks RACS

maintenance. In other words, through the AppFactory process, developers can deploy their Liquid applications on RACS. After verification, development, test and validation phases, their app will be packaged into a customized VM and it will be deployed on all the RACS.

Chapter 4.
Edge Computing Reference Architecture

Model-Driven Reference Architecture

The reference architecture is designed based on Model-Driven Engineering (MDE) principles. The model used for the reference architecture enables knowledge in the physical and digital worlds to be modelled to achieve:

- Coordination Between the Physical and Digital Worlds

A real-time, systematic cognitive model of the physical world is established. The status of the physical world is predicted, and the running of the physical world emulated in the digital world. This approach simplifies reconstruction of the physical world and drives the physical world to optimize the operation of physical systems. Full lifecycle data of the physical world can coordinate with business process data to enable collaboration between business and production processes.

- Cross-Industry Collaboration

Based on the modelling approach, the Information and Communications Technology (ICT) industry and vertical industries can build and reuse knowledge modelling systems in their own realms. The ICT industry shields the complexity of ICT technologies using the horizontal edge computing model and reference architecture. Each vertical industry performs modelling encapsulation of the industry know-how, achieving effective collaboration between ICT vendors and vertical industries.

- Reduced System Heterogeneity and Simplified Cross-Platform Migration

Model-based interfaces between systems, subsystems, services, and new and legacy systems enable interaction, simplifying integration of these systems. Using the model, software interfaces can be decoupled from development languages, platforms, tools, and protocols, which reduces the complexity of cross-platform migration.

- Effective Support for System Lifecycle Activities

System lifecycle activities include full lifecycle activities of application development services, deployment and operation services, data processing services, and security services.

The ICT industry faces challenges such as the need to simplify architectures, establish service intelligence and reduce Capital Expenditure (CAPEX) and Operating Expense (OPEX) in the areas of networking, computing, and storage. To address these challenges, the ICT industry is adopting technological innovations such as virtualization, Software-Defined Networking (SDN), model-driven Service Orchestrator (SO), and microservices. Edge computing is an Operation Technology (OT) and ICT convergence industry, and the edge computing reference architecture design needs to draw on the new technologies and concepts. In addition, edge computing and cloud computing coordinate with each other, yet differ in many ways. Therefore, edge computing faces unique challenges and requires unique and innovative technologies.

Based on the above concepts, the Edge Computing Consortium (ECC) proposes Edge Computing Reference Architecture 2.0.

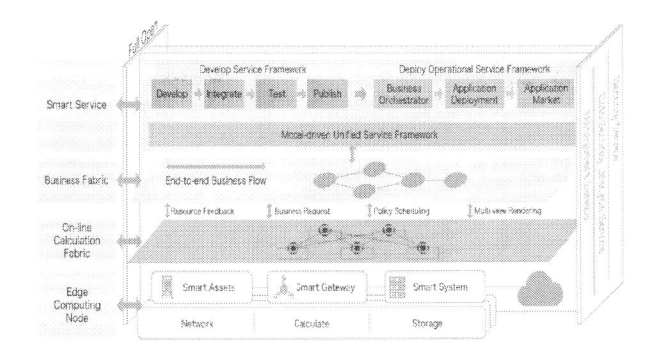

Figure 4.1: Edge computing reference architecture 2.0

From the horizontal perspective, the architecture has the following characteristics:

•   Smart services are based on the model-driven unified service framework. Intelligent coordination between service development and deployment is achieved through the development service framework and deployment & operation service framework. These frameworks enable consistent software development interfaces and automatic deployment and operations.

•   Smart service orchestration defines the E2E service flow through the service fabric (SF) to realize service agility.

•   Use of a Connectivity and Computing Fabric (CCF) enables a simplified architecture and simplifies the distributed edge intelligence architecture for services. The CCF also enables automatic and visualized deployment and operations of the OT & ICT (OICT) infrastructure, supporting coordination between edge computing resource services and service needs of industries.

•   Intelligent Edge Computing Nodes (ECNs) are compatible with a variety of heterogeneous connections, support real-time processing and response, and deliver integrated hardware and software security.

Edge Computing Reference Architecture 2.0 provides model-based open interfaces at each layer, enabling full-layer openness. Vertically, the architecture uses management services, lifecycle data services, and security services to deliver smart services in the entire service process and full lifecycle.

Multi-View Display
Guided by international standards defined by ISO/IEC/IEEE 42010:2011, the architecture systematically addresses the industry's concerns about edge computing and presents solutions and frameworks. Edge Computing Reference Architecture 2.0 is demonstrated using the following views:

• Concept View
Describes the domain models and key concepts of edge computing.

• Function View

35

Describes the functions and design concepts of the development service framework, deployment and operation framework SF, CCF, and ECN in the horizontal direction, as well as of cross-layer open services, management services, lifecycle data services, and security services in the vertical direction.

• Deployment View
Describes the system deployment process and typical deployment scenarios.

In addition, the architecture needs to meet typical cross-industry, non-functional requirements, including real-time performance, certainty, and reliability. To this end, related technical solution recommendations are provided in the function view and deployment view.

Concept View

Smart edge computing assets, systems, and gateways are digitalized, network-based, and intelligent. They provide ICT resources such as networks, computing, and storage, and can be logically abstracted as ECNs.

To suit the typical application scenarios of ECNs, the architecture defines four types of ECN development frameworks. Each framework includes an operating system, functional modules, and integrated development environment to meet the needs of various scenarios.

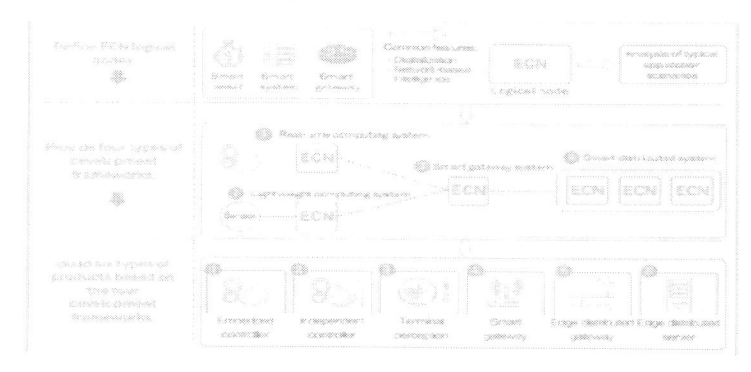

Figure 4.2: Concept view: ECNs, development frameworks, and product implementation

Typical functions of ECNs include:
- Bus protocol adaptation
- Real-time connection
- Streaming real-time data analysis
- Sequential data access
- Policy execution
- Device plug-and-play
- Resource management

Development frameworks of ECNs include:

• Real-Time Computing System
For digital physical assets; meets the needs of real-time applications.

• Lightweight Computing System
For sensing terminals with limited resources; meets the needs of low power consumption.

- **Smart Gateway System**
Supports multiple network interfaces, bus protocols, and network topologies; enables interconnection of local edge systems; delivers local computing and storage capabilities; and enables interworking with cloud systems.

- **Smart Distributed System**
Based on a distributed architecture, this framework flexibly expands network, computing, and storage capabilities at the network edge; supports service-oriented dynamic resource management and scheduling; and enables interworking with cloud systems.

ECN product implementation:	
Product	**Typical Scenario**
ICT-converged gateway	Connection of elevators, smart street lamp
Independent controller	Industrial Programmable Logic Controller (PLC)
Embedded controller	Virtual Programmable Logic Controller (vPLC), robot
Sensing terminal	Computer Numerical Control (CNC), instrument
Distributed service gateway	Smart power distribution
Edge cluster (edge cloud)	Digital workshop

Edge Computing Domain Models

Edge computing domain models are defined from the ICT perspective of edge computing.

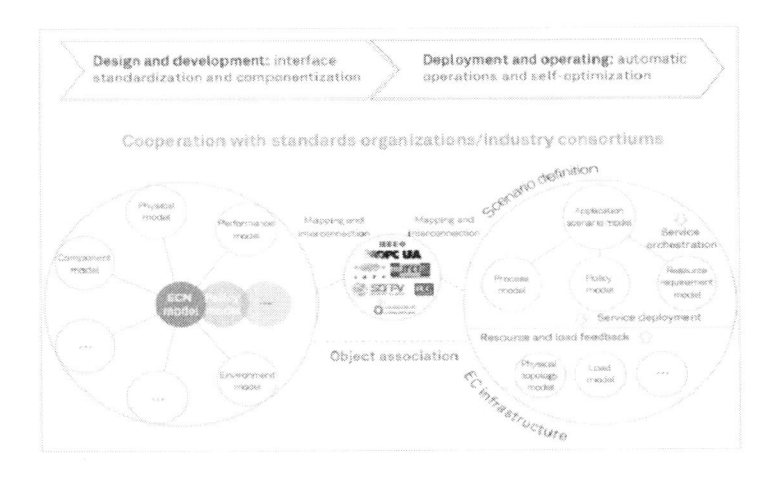

Figure 4.3: Concept view: full lifecycle-oriented models

• Models in the Design Phase
Define the IDs, attributes, functions, performance, and derivation and inheritance relationships of ECNs, providing valuable information for the deployment and operation phases.

• Models in the Deployment Phase
Include service policy and physical topology models. The service policy model describes service rules and constraints using a service language rather than machine language, allowing services to drive the edge computing infrastructure. The service policy model is reusable and changeable, enabling service agility.

• Models in the Operation Phase
Include the connection computing fabric model and operation load model. Based on these models, the system operating status can be monitored and optimized, and the deployment of loads optimized on the distributed edge architecture.

Through the model-driven unified service framework, edge computing domain models and vertical industry models can be mapped to each other and centrally managed. In this way, vertical industry models such as OPC Unified Architecture (OPC UA) and its ecosystem can be reused, allowing for easy integration of the edge computing reference architecture with industry platforms and applications.

Function View

ECN

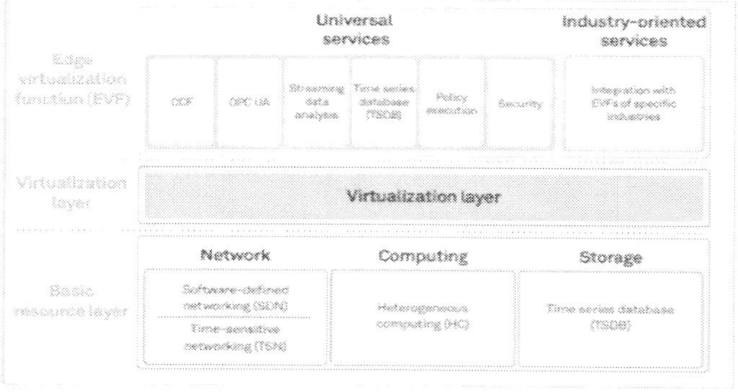

Figure 4.4: Function view: ECN functional layers

Virtualization Layer		Virtualization layer	
	Network	Computing	Storage
Basic resource layer	Software-defined networking (SDN)	Heterogeneous computing (HC)	Time series database (TSDB)
	Time-sensitive networking (TSN)		

1) Basic Resource Layer
This layer includes network, computing and storage modules.

• Network
SDN architectures separate a network's control plane from the forwarding plane to make the network programmable. When SDN is applied to edge computing, the network can support access to millions of network devices as well as flexible expansion, enabling efficient and low-cost automatic O&M. Additionally, this approach helps achieve network and security policy association and integration.

Network connections need to accommodate requirements for transmission time certainty and data integrity. Time-Sensitive Networking (TSN) series standards define unified technical specifications for key services such as real-time priorities and clocks. TSN is the future development direction of industrial Ethernet connectivity.

• Computing
Heterogeneous Computing (HC) is a crucial aspect of the computing hardware architecture at the network edge. Even as Moore's Law continues to hold true for breakthroughs in chip technologies, the popularity of IoT applications has brought explosive growth in information volume, and the application of Artificial Intelligence (AI) has increased computing complexity. These developments place higher requirements on computing capabilities. The types of data to be processed are also becoming more diversified. As a result, edge devices need to process both structured and unstructured data. In addition, as ECNs contain more compute units and different types of compute units, costs become a concern.

Therefore, a new computing architecture is proposed that combines compute units that handle different types of instruction sets and have different architectures, that is, heterogeneous computing. Such an architecture gives full play to the advantages of various compute units, achieving a balance between performance, cost, power consumption, and portability.

Additionally, a new generation of AI technology, represented by deep learning, needs new technical optimizations at the network edge. Currently, the processing of a single picture at the inference stage often requires more than 1 billion computations, so standard deep learning algorithms are obviously not suitable for embedded computing environments at the network edge. Ongoing optimization for deep learning in the industry includes top-down optimization, which compresses learned deep-learning models to reduce computational load at the inference stage. Bottom-up optimization that redefines an algorithm architecture oriented for edge-side embedded system environment is also being attempted.

• Storage
The digital world needs to keep track of the dynamics of the physical world in real time and store complete historical data in chronological order. A new generation of Time Series Database (TSDB) offers efficient storage for time series data (including information such as timestamps of the data). TSDBs need to support basic functions of time series data, such as fast write, persistence, and multi-dimensional aggregated query. To ensure data accuracy and completeness, TSDBs need to continuously add new time series data instead of updating the original data. These requirements raise the following challenges:

• The time series data write function must support writing tens or hundreds of millions of data points per second.

• The time series data read function must support packet aggregation operations on hundreds of millions of data values within seconds.

• The cost-sensitive nature of most scenarios means that the top priority of TSDBs is to reduce the cost of mass data storage.

2) Virtualization Layer
Virtualization technology reduces system development and deployment costs, and has been adopted into embedded system applications from server applications. Typical virtualization technologies include the bare metal architecture and host architecture. In the bare metal architecture, virtualization-layer functions such as the hypervisor run directly on the system hardware platform, and then operating system and virtualization functions run under the hypervisor. In the host architecture, virtualization-layer functions run under the host operating system. The bare metal architecture has better real-time performance and is generally used by smart assets and smart gateways.

3) EVF Layer
Edge Virtualization Functions (EVFs) are software-based and service-based functions that are decoupled from a proprietary hardware platform. Based on virtualization technology, the hardware, system, and specific EVFs can be vertically combined based on services on the same hardware platform. In this manner, multiple independent service zones can be virtualized and isolated from each other. ECN's EVF service scalability reduces CAPEX and extends a system's lifecycle.

EVFs can be flexibly combined and orchestrated, and migrated and expanded on different hardware platforms and devices, enabling dynamic resource scheduling and service agility.

The EVF layer delivers the following basic services that can be tailored:
- Distributed CCF service
- OPC UA service
- Streaming real-time data analysis service
- TSDB service
- Policy execution service
- Security service

Key ECN Technologies:

1) SDN
SDN uses a completely different control architecture from traditional networks. It separates the network control plane from the forwarding plane, replaces the original distributed control with centralized control, and implements "software-defined" through open, programmable interfaces. SDN, as a new technology, changes the way a network is built and operated: building networks from an application perspective and operating networks using Information Technology (IT).

The SDN architecture includes controllers, southbound/northbound interfaces, and various application-layer applications and infrastructure-layer Network Elements (NEs). The most important part of the architecture is the SDN controller. It implements configuration and management of forwarding policies at the infrastructure layer and supports forwarding control based on multiple flow tables.

SDN's unique benefits for edge computing include:

• Mass Connections
SDN supports access to millions of network devices and flexible expansion. SDN also integrates and adapts to the management of multi-vendor network devices.

• Model-Driven Policy Automation
SDN provides flexible network automation and management frameworks; enables service-based infrastructure and service delivery functions; and implements plug-and-play smart assets, gateways, and systems. These capabilities greatly reduce the technical requirements for network administrators.

• E2E Service Protection

SDN delivers E2E tunnel services, such as Generic Routing Encapsulation (GRE), Layer 2 Tunneling Protocol (L2TP), Internet Protocol Security (IPSec), and Virtual Extensible LAN (VXLAN). SDN also optimizes Quality of Service (QoS) scheduling, helps meet key requirements such as E2E bandwidth and delay specifications, and implements edge-to-cloud service coordination.

• Lifecycle Management of Applications

SDN supports lifecycle management tasks such as application deployment, loading, update, uninstallation, and deletion. SDN also supports multi-application resource scheduling and management, including priority enforcement, security, and QoS.

• Architecture Openness

SDN opens centralized network control and network status information to smart applications so that they can flexibly and quickly drive network resource scheduling.

Edge computing SDN technology has been successfully applied to smart buildings, smart elevators, and many other industry scenarios.

2) TSN

Standard Ethernet technologies have been widely implemented, with advantages such as high transmission speed, flexible topology, long transmission distance, and cost-effectiveness. Meanwhile, due to constraints from the traditional Quality of Service (QoS) mechanism and the Carrier Sense Multiple Access with Collision Detection (CSMA/CD) mechanism, Ethernet technologies cannot meet key industry requirements for timeliness and determinism. The industry optimizes standard Ethernet technologies and offers commercial implementations of multiple industrial real-time Ethernet technologies. Consequently, a variety of industrial real-time Ethernet networks coexist, creating obstacles and challenges for interoperation.

In recent years, IEEE802.1 defined the TSN technical standards, aiming to promote standardization and interoperability of real-time Ethernet networks, and ultimately merging Operational Technologies (OT) and ICT using 'one network.' This also brings the following advantages:

• Ensures determinism with μs-level latency and jitter of less than 500 ns.

• Meets large bandwidth requirements for scenarios such as industrial machine vision, with interface bandwidth of larger than 1 Gbit/s.

• Achieves reliable data transmission through multiple paths or redundant paths.

• Coordinates with SDN technologies to achieve unified scheduling management of TSN and non-TSN networks.

TSN is designed to provide a unified low-latency queue scheduling mechanism, resource reservation mechanism, clock synchronization mechanism, path control mechanism, and configuration management model at the Media Access Control (MAC) layer of Ethernet networks, to achieve interoperation between TSN networks and standard Ethernet networks.

Currently, a good industrial collaboration ecosystem for TSN has been established. For example, IEEE is responsible for standards establishment, Avnu Alliance is responsible for interoperability certification, and industrial organizations represented by the ECC and the Industrial Internet Consortium (IIC) are performing industry demonstrations and promotion through test beds and other activities.

3) HC

Heterogeneous computing architecture is designed to coordinate and bring into play unique advantages of various computing units: The Central Processing Unit (CPU) manages system control, task decomposition, and scheduling; the Graphics Processing Unit (GPU) has strong floating-point and vector computing capabilities, and performs well with parallel computing such as matrix computing and vector computing; the Field Programmable Gate Array (FPGA) unit provides advantages such as hardware programmability and low latency; the Application-Specific Integrated Circuit (ASIC) unit offers advantages such as low power consumption, high performance, and cost-effectiveness.

The objective of heterogeneous computing is to integrate separate processing units of the same platform to collaboratively execute different types of computing loads. Moreover, heterogeneous computing achieves cross-platform deployment of software through open, unified programmable interfaces.

The heterogeneous computing architecture uses the following key technologies:

• Memory processing optimization
With a traditional architecture, data transfer between different computing units requires data replication, which not only occupies processor resources, but also occupies a large amount of system bus bandwidth. Heterogeneous computing enables uniform memory access of multiple computing units. Data of any processing unit can be easily accessed by other processing units, without the need of copying the data to each other's memory area, which greatly improves system performance.

• Task scheduling optimization
The relationship of various computing units changes from master-slave relationship to equal partnership. The most appropriate computing unit is dynamically determined to execute the workload based on tasks. Heterogeneous computing involves a series of optimizations, including those of scheduling algorithms, instruction sets, and compilers.

• Tool chain for development
The tool chain provides application programmers with hardware and software interfaces as well as a basic runtime environment; encapsulates and hides complicated bottom-layer details such as memory consistency and task scheduling management; supports optimization of architecture parameters and task scheduling; and minimizes the application porting workload. For Artificial Intelligence (AI) applications, this tool chain integrates multiple open AI training and reasoning platforms and is compatible with multi-vendor computing units.

Heterogeneous computing is currently used in both chip design and edge computing platform design. In terms of chips, heterogeneous computing integrates CPU and GPU resources to accelerate video encoding and decoding. In terms of computing platforms, heterogeneous computing uses CPU and FPGA (or GPU) resources to achieve implementation of AI functions in areas such as smart transportation and smart robots.

4) Time Series Database (TSDB)

Efficient writing, query, and distributed storage of large amounts of data are key challenges to TSDBs. TSDBs use the following key technologies:

• Distributed storage
The core for distributed storage is how to distribute data to multiple machines, that is, data fragmentation. Data fragmentation can be implemented based on timestamps, tags, and priorities. Data fragments that have the same tag (one or more identical fields), are generated within the same time range, and matching priority conditions are stored on the same machine. Data can be compressed before it is stored, which improves data writing efficiency and saves storage space.

• Priority-based storage
Using timestamps of time series data as the priority division basis is very efficient. Data that

was processed recently is queried for more times and is considered hot data. Data that was processed a long time ago is queried less often and is considered cold data. In addition, factors such as storage costs are often considered in priority-based storage. Data with different priorities is stored on storage media with different costs (including memories, HDDs, and SSDs).

• Fragment-based query optimization
During data queries, all data segments are queried based on query conditions. All of the fragments are merged based upon the timestamp conditions to generate the original data results. If the query conditions include aggregation operations on data, these operations are performed based on the time sampling window for returning the results.

Besides commercial versions, the industry has a large number of open-source TSDBs, such as OpenTSDB, KairosDB, and InfluxDB. In addition to meeting performance challenges, TSDBs need to provide industry data modelling and visualization tools and to support rapid integration with industry application systems.

Service Fabric

A service fabric is a model-based workflow that digitally represents service requirements. It consists of multiple types of logically related functional services that collaborate with each other to implement specific service requirements.
The service model includes the following information:
- Service name
- Function to be executed or provided
- Nesting, dependency, and inheritance relationships between services
- Input and output of each service
- Service constraints such as QoS, security, and reliability

The service types include universal services provided by edge computing and specific industry services defined by vertical industries.

A service fabric has the following features:
- Focus on service processes and shield technical details, helping service departments, development departments, and deployment operation departments establish effective cooperation.
- Decouple from the OICT infrastructure and hardware platform to implement cross-technology platforms and support service agility.
- As a service description model, it can be inherited and reused to implement fast modelling.

A service fabric provides the following functions:
- Workflow and workload definition
- Visualized display
- Semantic check and policy conflict detection
- Version management of fabric and service models

CCF

The CCF is a virtualized connectivity and computing service layer. It has the following features:

- Shield the heterogeneity between ECNs.
- Reduce the complexity of the smart distributed architecture in terms of data consistency and error tolerance.
- Implement the discovery, unified management, and orchestration of resource services.

- Support the sharing of data and knowledge models between ECNs.
- Support dynamic scheduling and optimization of the service load.
- Support distributed decision-making and policy execution.

Figure 4.5: Function view: CCF

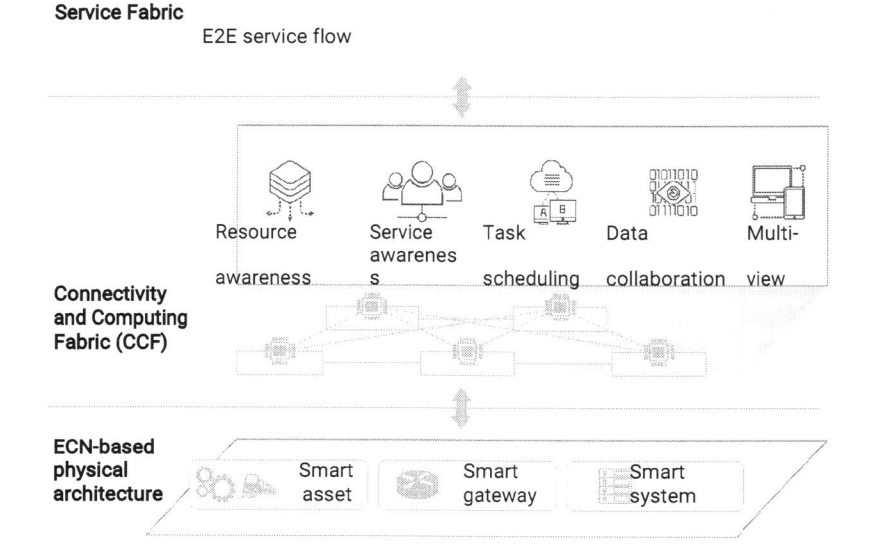

Service Fabric

E2E service flow

Connectivity and Computing Fabric (CCF): Resource awareness, Service awareness, Task scheduling, Data collaboration, Multi-view

ECN-based physical architecture: Smart asset, Smart gateway, Smart system

A CCF provides the following functions:

a. Resource awareness
The CCF can detect the ICT resource status (such as network connection quality and CPU usage), performance specifications (such as real-time performance), and physical information (such as location) of each ECN, providing key input for resource allocation and scheduling at the edge.

b. EVF awareness
The CCF can detect the EVFs provided by the system, ECNs where the EVFs are distributed, computing tasks that each EVF serves, and task execution status.

c. Workload scheduling
The CCF supports proactive task scheduling. It can automatically divide the workload into multiple subtasks based on resource awareness, service awareness, and service constraints (such as the connection bandwidth and delay requirement between ECNs) and allocate them to multiple ECNs for collaborative computing. In addition, the CCF can open the resource and service information for the service fabrics through open interfaces so that the service fabrics can automatically control the scheduling process of the workload.

d. Data collaboration
ECNs adapt to the southbound multi-bus protocol. The east-west connections between ECNs use a unified data connection protocol. Through data collaboration, ECNs can exchange data and knowledge models with each other. The exchange modes include simple broadcast and Pub/Sub.

e. Multi-view display
Services can be displayed by tenant or service logic, shielding physical connection complexity. For example, each tenant only needs to view its own workload, distribution of the workload on the CCF, and resource usage.

f. Open service interfaces
The CCF provides workload requests, resource status feedback, and scheduling and execution status feedback through open interfaces to shield physical differences between smart assets, smart gateways, and smart systems.

Development Service Framework (Smart Service)

Figure 4.6: Function view: development service framework

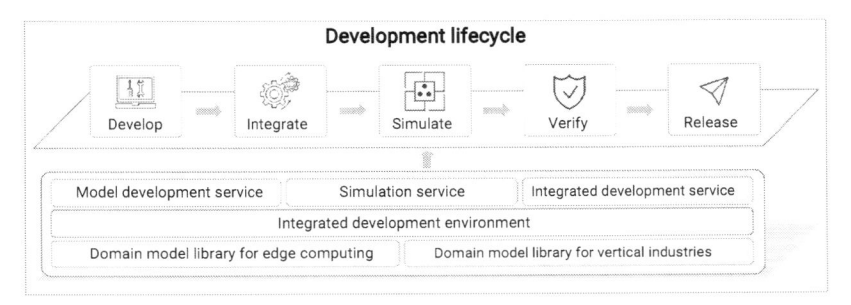

Development lifecycle

Develop → Integrate → Simulate → Verify → Release

| Model development service | Simulation service | Integrated development service |

Integrated development environment

| Domain model library for edge computing | Domain model library for vertical industries |

The edge computing model library and vertical industry model library are integrated through the integrated development platform and tool chain to provide full-lifecycle services for the development, integration, simulation, verification, and release of models and apps.

The development service framework supports the following key services:

a. Model-based development service

• Support model definitions including the architecture, function requirements, and interface requirements.

• Support visualized display of the model and service processes.

• Support generation of multi-language codes based on models.

• Support integration and mapping of the edge computing domain models and vertical industry domain models.

• Support model library version management.

b. Emulation service

• Support software and hardware simulation of ECNs, allowing the specifications such as memory and storage space of ECNs to be simulated in the target application scenarios. The system needs to support fine-grained componentization and component tailoring and re-packaging (system reset) to match ECN specifications.

• Based on simulation nodes, build networks and systems based on application scenarios, and perform low-cost and automated function verification on the developed models and apps in a simulation environment.

c. Integrated release service
• Obtain the release version from the baseline library, invoke the deployment operation service, and deploy the models and apps to real ECNs.

Deployment Operation Service Framework (Smart Service)

The framework includes the following key services: service orchestration, app deployment (not prescribed in this document), and app market.

1) Service orchestration service
Generally, the service orchestration service is based on a three-layer architecture.

Figure 4.7 :Function view: service orchestration layer

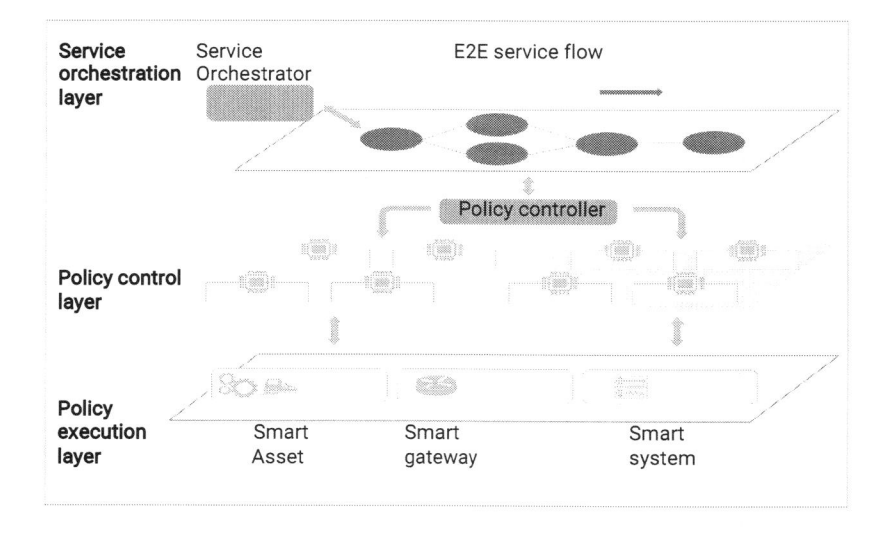

• Service orchestrator
The orchestrator defines service fabrics, which are generally deployed on the cloud (public or private cloud) or local systems (smart systems). The orchestrator provides a visualized workflow definition tool and supports Create/Retrieve/Update/Delete (CRUD) operations. The orchestrator can orchestrate services based on the service templates and policy templates defined by the development service framework and reuse the templates. Before delivering a service fabric to the policy controller, the orchestrator can perform semantic check and policy conflict detection on the workflow.

• Policy controller
To ensure real-time service scheduling and control, the policy controller is deployed at the network edge to implement local control.

Based on certain policies and the services and capabilities supported by the local CCFs, the policy controller allocates the service flows defined by a service fabric to a local CCF for scheduling and execution.

Because the edge computing domain and vertical industry domain require different domain knowledge and system implementation, the controller design and deployment are generally implemented by domain. The edge computing domain controller is responsible for deploying edge computing services such as security and data analysis. If the vertical industry service logic is involved, the vertical industry domain controller is responsible for distribution and scheduling.

• Policy executor
Each ECN has a built-in policy executor, which is responsible for translating policies into local device commands and performing local scheduling and execution. ECNs can either passively receive policies delivered by the controller or proactively request policies from the controller.

The policies need to focus only on high-level service requirements without implementing fine-grained control on ECNs. This ensures the autonomy of ECNs and real-time responses to local events.

2) App market service
The app market service connects consumers and suppliers, and can transform the unilateral innovation of an enterprise into the multilateral open innovation in an industry ecosystem. Suppliers can encapsulate the industry know-how into apps and register them with the app market for quick publishing. Consumers can easily find an app matching their requirements from the app catalogue and subscribe to the app.

The app market service supports a wide range of apps, including the mechanism models constructed based on industrial knowledge, algorithm models constructed based on data analysis methods, service fabric models that can be inherited and reused, and apps that support specific functions (such as fault diagnosis). These apps can be directly used by end users or used for secondary development through model-based open interfaces.

Management Service

• Support the unified management service oriented to terminals, network devices, servers, storage, data, isolation between services and apps, security, and distributed architecture.

• Support the full-lifecycle management of engineering design, integration design, system deployment, service and data migration, integration testing, and integration verification and acceptance.

Full-Lifecycle Data Service

1) Edge data characteristics
Edge data is generated at the network edge and includes machine running data, environment data, and information system data. It features high throughput (large transient traffic), fast flow movement, diversity, strong correlation, and high requirements on real-time analysis and processing.

Compared with business big data scenarios such as Internet, smart analysis of edge data has the following characteristics and differences:

• Causal relationship vs. association relationship
Edge data is mainly targeted at smart assets that generally run with explicit input and output causal relationships, whereas business big data focuses on data association relationships.

• High reliability vs. low reliability
Industries such as manufacturing and transportation have high requirements on the accuracy and reliability of models. If the accuracy or reliability is low, property loss or even personal injury may occur. In contrast, business big data analysis generally has low requirements on reliability. It is required that the edge data analysis result be explainable. Therefore, black-box deep learning is restricted in some application scenarios. The combination of the traditional mechanism models and data analysis methods is the innovation and application direction of smart analysis.

- Small data vs. big data

Assets such as machine tools and vehicles are designed and manufactured by people. Most data in their running process is predictable, and only data generated in abnormal or critical conditions is truly valuable. On the other hand, business big data analysis requires mass data.

2) Full-lifecycle data service

Service fabrics are used to define the full-lifecycle data service logic, including specifying the data analysis algorithms. CCFs are used to optimize the data service deployment and running to meet real-time service requirements.

The full-lifecycle data service includes the following:

- Data pre-processing

Filter, clean, aggregate, and optimize (including dirty data elimination) raw data and perform semantic parsing.
- Data analysis
- Based on streaming data analysis, process data in real time so that events and ever-changing service conditions and requirements can be responded to quickly, accelerating the continuous analysis of data.
- Provide the common statistical model library and support the algorithm integration of models such as statistical models and mechanism models.
- Support model training methods such as lightweight deep learning.
- Data distribution and policy execution.

Execute policies locally based on predefined rules and data analysis results, or forward data to the cloud or other ECNs for processing.

- Data visualization and storage

Using technologies such as TSDB can significantly conserve storage space and meet the requirements on high-speed read and write operations. Next-generation interaction technologies such as AR and VR are used to provide a vivid display effect.

Security Service

The security design and implementation of the edge computing architecture are first expected to provide the following features:

- Security functions adapt to the specific architecture of edge computing.
- Security functions can be flexibly deployed and expanded.
- The system can continuously mitigate attacks within a certain period of time.
- The system can tolerate function failures to a certain extent and within a specified range, while basic functions run properly.
- The entire system can quickly recover from failure.

In addition, the security design and implementation need to take the following unique features of edge computing scenarios into consideration:

- Lightweight security functions can be deployed on IoT devices with limited hardware resources.
- The traditional trust-based security model is no longer applicable to the access of a large number of heterogeneous devices. Therefore, the security model (such as the whitelist function) needs to be re-designed based on the minimum authorization principle.
- Isolation between networks and domains is implemented on key nodes (such as smart gateways) to control the scope of security attacks and risks, preventing attacks on a node from spreading to the entire network.
- The security and real-time situation awareness functions are seamlessly embedded

into the entire edge computing architecture to achieve continuous detection and response. Automation should be implemented as much as possible, but manual intervention is also required at times.

Security design must cover each layer of the edge computing architecture, and different layers require different security features. In addition, unified situation awareness, security management and orchestration, identity authentication and management, and security O&M are required to ensure maximum security and reliability of the entire architecture.

Figure 4.8: Function view: security service

Security Situation Awareness		Security O&M and Orchestration	
Big-Data Security Analyse (Awareness)		Proactive Protection	
APT Detection	Correlation Analysis	Application Orchestration Security	Security Service Lifecycle Mgmt.
Threat Tracing	Security Compliance Audit	Resource Pool Mgmt. Security	Unified Security Policies and Orchestration

Whitelist	Malicious Code Prevention	Security Configuration WAF	Security Detection and Repose
Application Security Audit	Software Hardening and Patch	Security Configuration and Mgmt.	Sandbox

Data Isolation/Destruction	Data Tamper-proof		
Encryption	Private Protection	Data Access Control	DLP

Reuse of Transport Protocols Security Features (REST)			
Firewall	IPS/IDS	**AntiDDoS**	VPN/TLS

Secure/Reliable Remote Upgrade	Lightweight Trusted Computing		
ECN Security	Hardware Safety	Software Hardening and Security Configuration	

ECN security: Includes basic ECN security, endpoint security, software hardening and security configuration, secure and reliable remote upgrade, lightweight trusted computing, and hardware safety switch. Secure and reliable remote upgrade can fix vulnerabilities, install patches in time and prevent system failures after the upgrade. Lightweight trusted computing is applicable to simple IoT devices with limited computing (CPU) and storage resources to solve basic trust problems.

Network (fabric) security: Includes firewalls, IPS/IDS, anti-DDoS, VPN/TLS, and the reuse of security functions of some transport protocols, such as the REST protocol. Anti-DDoS is particularly important in IoT and edge computing. In recent years, a growing number of attacks on IoT devices are DDoS attacks. Attackers control IoT devices with poor security (such as cameras with fixed passwords) to attack specific targets.

Data security: Includes data encryption, data isolation and destruction, data anti-tampering, privacy protection (data anonymization), data access control, and data leakage prevention. Data encryption includes encryption during data transmission and storage. Data leakage prevention for edge computing is different from that of traditional systems because edge computing devices are usually deployed in distributed mode. Special considerations are required to ensure that data will not be leaked even if these devices are stolen.

Application security: Includes security functions such as whitelist, application security audit, malicious code prevention, web application firewall (WAF), and sandbox. The whitelist function is important in the edge computing architecture. The traditional trust-based security model is no longer applicable to the access of a large number of heterogeneous terminals and various services. Therefore, security models (such as the whitelist function) with minimal authorization are used to manage applications and access rights.

Security situation awareness and security management and orchestration: Since a large number of diversified terminals are connected at the network edge and services carried on the network are complex, passive security defence is ineffective. Therefore, more proactive security defence methods are required, including Big Data–based situation awareness, advanced threat detection, unified network-wide security policy execution, and proactive protection. These can facilitate quick responses. In combination with comprehensive O&M monitoring and emergency response mechanisms, maximum security, availability, and reliability of the edge computing architecture can be ensured.

Identity and authentication management: Covers all function layers. However, accessing a large number of devices at the network edge places much pressure on the performance of the traditional centralized security authentication system, especially when many devices go online within a short period of time. Therefore, the decentralized and distributed authentication and certificate management can be used if needed.

Deployment View

The edge computing architecture provides the following typical deployment models: three-layer model and four-layer model.

1) Three-layer deployment model

This model is applicable to scenarios where services are deployed in one or more scattered areas, each with a low traffic volume.

Typical scenarios include smart street lamps, smart elevators, and smart environmental protection.

After local processing of smart assets, multiple types are offered, multiple service data flows are aggregated on the smart gateways along the north-south direction. In addition to network functions such as supporting the access and local management of smart assets and bus protocol conversion, the smart gateways provide real-time streaming data analysis, security protection, and small-scale data storage. The gateways process real-time service requirements locally, and aggregate and send non-real-time data to the cloud for processing.

2) Four-layer deployment model

This model is applicable to scenarios where services are deployed centrally and the traffic volume is high.

Typical scenarios include smart video analysis, distributed grid, and smart manufacturing.

The typical differences between four-layer deployment and three-layer deployment are as follows: At the edge, there is a large amount of data and many local application systems are deployed. Therefore, a large amount of computing and storage resources are required. After most real-time data processing is completed on smart assets and smart gateways, data is aggregated on local distributed smart systems for secondary processing. The distributed ECNs exchange data and knowledge through east-west connections, support horizontal elastic expansion of computing and storage resources, and implement real-time decision-making and optimization operations locally.

Chapter 5.
Edge Computing & IoT

IoT market analysts expect the edge to play a significant role in supporting IoT implementations going forward, as it creates efficiencies and scale in networks that makes IoT deployments more self-sustaining. IDC (International Data Corporation) estimates that by 2020, IT spending on edge infrastructure will reach up to 18 per cent of the total spend on IoT infrastructure.[1] Mobile operators have the demonstrable capability to manage infrastructure, data and applications for IoT services, and are well placed to continue this with edge for IoT.

Rapidly increasing numbers of IoT devices and resultant data mean that new techniques to meet customer requirements and ensure effective management need to be explored. Alternatives to the traditional IoT model of sending all data to the cloud for processing are required as the volume of data to be processed explodes, and the cost of centrally storing and processing every piece of data, important or not, becomes harder to justify. This is particularly important for IoT services, as they can generate large volumes of new data for analysis. Edge computing is a deployment model which aims to push the relevant data processing and storage attributes closer to where the device is located. This means that data can be processed more efficiently, and many attributes do not need to be centralised. Mobile operators are well placed to enable edge computing to scale and enhance IoT deployments, additionally allowing options for data processing on behalf of customers to be further incorporated into their service offerings.

However, implementation of edge computing for IoT by mobile operators is not without challenges.
New investments, infrastructure and management platforms may be needed. Today, edge computing is a relatively immature technology that has been dominated by traditional cloud providers. Other members of the IoT ecosystem, including mobile operators, do have roles to play but as the IoT is still evolving, it will take some time for appropriate commercial and technical models to emerge.

This chapter explores the benefits to the IoT of edge computing and some of the different use cases where it could be applied. It explores the potential operator role for IoT edge computing and identifies some potential next steps to be undertaken by the industry.

IoT reference model

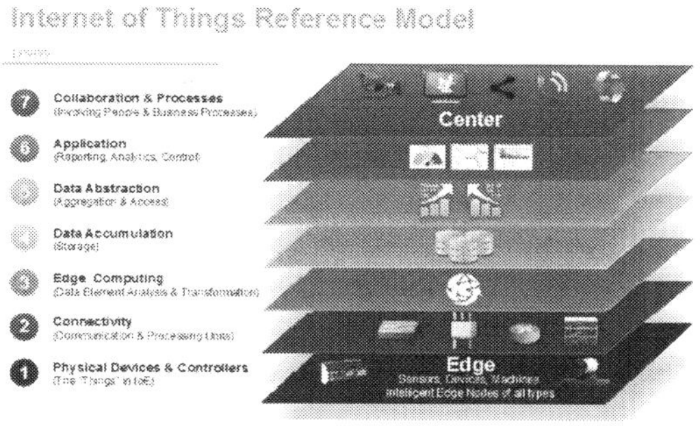

Figure 5.1: IoT reference model (cisco 2014)

IOT reference model contains broadly seven layers. Researchers have different opinions about the number of reference layers; it varies from 3 to 7.

Physical Devices and Controllers
This layer has physical devices like sensors for sensing and assembling information about the surroundings which senses some physical parameters or identifies other smart objects in the environment.

Connectivity
In connectivity layer, communications and processing are executed by existing networks. This layer includes connectors like RJ45, ModBus, USB or wireless connectivity.

Computing
The objective of computing layer is for mainly analysing of data and data formation. Data is prepared by encoding, decoding, summarizing and transformation of data. This layer is also known as edge computing.

Data Accumulation
Data storage and data functionality are handled in this layer. This considers type of data, processing of data, higher level application data compatibility, combining of data and storage type. In the area of huge Data backend Hadoop, HBase, MongoDB, and Cassandra can be added for data storage.

Data Abstraction
The data abstraction layer receives data, sent from the devices stored at data accumulation layer and then sends to an endpoint to be used by the application. This sentence is not clear. The collected data is in many different formats as collected from different sources; it needs to be converted in the same format suitable for higher-level application. Data is indexed, normalized and provided with appropriate authentication and authorization for security.

Application (Reporting, Analytics, Control)
The main objective of the application layer is information interpretation and Software for interactions with previous data abstraction level. Simple communications applications can be handled like Mobile Applications are based on device data, business, programming patterns, and software stacks, operating systems, mobility, application servers, hypervisors, multi-threading, multi-tenancy, etc.

Collaboration and Processes (Involving people and business processes)
The information generated in IOT yields to accomplish in this layer by handover to end user and processes. They use applications and associated data for their specific requirements. Sixth layer Applications layer gives the right data at the right time, so they can do the right thing. People must be able to communicate and collaborate, sometimes using the traditional Internet, to make the IoT useful.

Mobile operators should view IoT edge computing as a flexible, distributed processing point beyond the core where network control, application logic, device management and data processing and analytics can be separated to enable a wide variety of deployment models along with automated and efficient management of IoT devices and data.

Location of the IoT edge from a mobile operator point of view

Figure 5.2: The Mobile Operator Edge

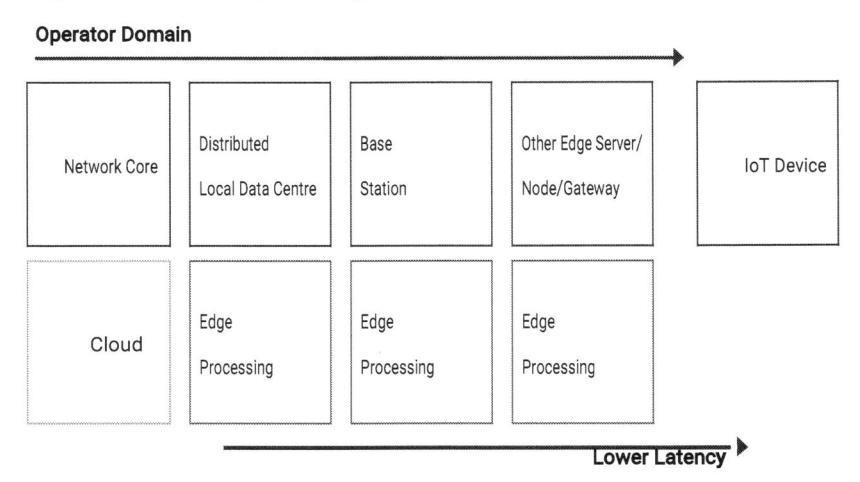

Operator Domain

Network Core	Distributed Local Data Centre	Base Station	Other Edge Server/ Node/Gateway	IoT Device
Cloud	Edge Processing	Edge Processing	Edge Processing	

Lower Latency ▶

Key Benefits of Edge for the IoT

Edge for the IoT brings potential benefits for many IoT deployments, including decreased response time along with increased communications efficiency, compared to using the cloud to process and store data. For example, many IoT processes can have a high level of automation at the edge resulting in low latency for rapid data processing. Only the most important information need then be sent to the cloud for further action or investigation.

Many new IoT services, such as intelligent vehicles, drones or smart grids, could come to rely on edge computing. Many of the benefits of IoT edge will need to be refined in proof of concept deployments by mobile operators to demonstrate that the model is beneficial. Benefits of IoT edge computing that have been identified include:

1. Low latency
By its nature, the edge is closer to the IoT device than the core or cloud. This means a shorter round-trip for communications to reach local processing power, significantly speeding up data communications and processing.

2. Longer battery life for IoT devices
Being able to open communication channels for shorter periods of time due to improved latency means that battery life of battery powered IoT devices could be extended. Distributed ledger, or a hybrid open source ledger implementation such as BigchainDB could be used to obtain the advantage of a distributed ledger which provides features from the NoSQL database MongoDB on which it is based.

3. More efficient data management
Processing data at the edge makes simple data quality management such as filtering and prioritisation more efficient. Completing this data administration at the edge, means cleaner data sets can be presented to cloud based processing for further analytics.

4. Access to data analytics and AI
Edge processing power and data storage could all be combined to enable analytics and AI, which require very fast response times or involve the processing of large 'real-time' data sets that are impractical to send to centralised systems.

5. Resilience
The edge offers more possible communication paths than a centralised model. This distribution means that resilience of data communications is more assured. If there is a failure at the edge, other resources are available to provide continuous operation.

6. Scalability
As processing is decentralised with the edge model, less load should ultimately be placed on the network. This means that scaling IoT devices should have less resource impact on the network, especially if application and control planes are located at the edge alongside the data.

Unique Requirements of Edge for the IoT

IoT edge requirements are different from non-IoT edge computing use cases. The IoT needs to support a large number of devices, many of which do not have their own dedicated data processing resources, but that may be generating a large volume of data.

The relationship between these devices and the edge is different from that of other connected devices such as smartphones, where much of the data processing can be completed on the device. In non-IoT use cases, the edge is often used to serve constant volumes of data to the end device so that to enable services such as video streaming or offer low latency applications for VR and gaming.

DIFFERENCES BETWEEN EDGE FOR IoT AND NON-IoT

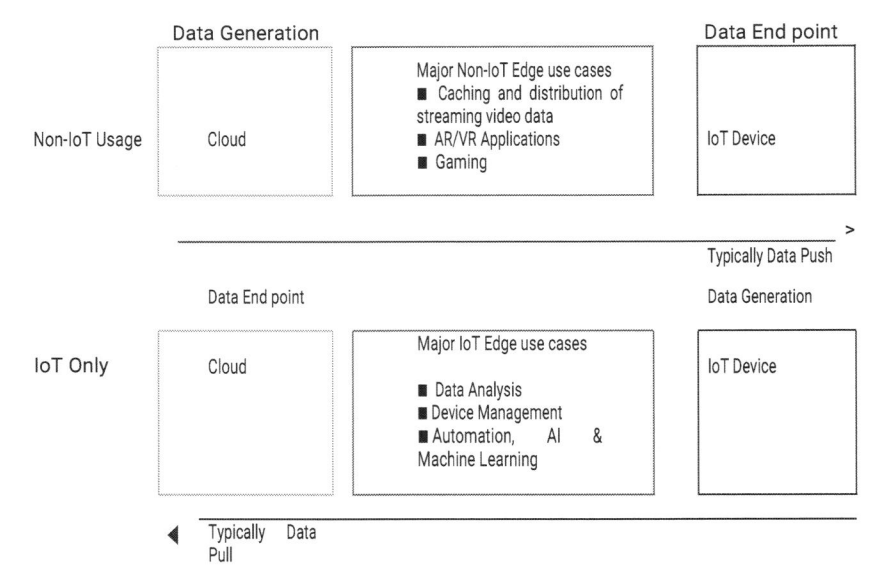

	Data Generation		Data End point
Non-IoT Usage	Cloud	Major Non-IoT Edge use cases ■ Caching and distribution of streaming video data ■ AR/VR Applications ■ Gaming	IoT Device

Typically Data Push →

	Data End point		Data Generation
IoT Only	Cloud	Major IoT Edge use cases ■ Data Analysis ■ Device Management ■ Automation, AI & Machine Learning	IoT Device

◄ Typically Data Pull

For some customers, the IoT and other services will possibly share the same physical infrastructure and enablement platforms as non-IoT services. This means that considerations for the IoT need to be taken in the deployment of any edge infrastructure. If the IoT is to share edge resources with non-IoT services, then it may be necessary to have dedicated resources allocated on the edge node or gateway to support required levels of service. IoT services often run 24/7 while other edge use cases may only run intensively at peak times of day. Therefore, there needs to be consideration of the scope of IoT requirements on resources to ensure they can be met, even at peak times.

Use Case for IoT Edge

The following use cases have been identified as some of those which may be able to benefit from IoT edge computing to improve the level of service for IoT devices and applications.

Category	IoT Foundation Supporting general IoT functionality	IoT Service Enablers Adding value to IoT	IoT Solutions Supporting customer solutions
Use Case	Device Management Security	Priority Messaging Data Aggregation Data Replication Cloud Enablement	IoT Image and Audio Processing

IoT Foundation

Device Management

There are many device attributes and configurations that can be controlled at the edge, with many device management platforms extending their functionality to manage devices connected to edge infrastructure. Below are examples of four different attributes that device management at the edge will need to support:

Distributed firmware updates – the use of the edge gateway to distribute firmware updates locally, with distribution being managed by the edge node as opposed to the queuing system typically used when a firmware update is distributed centrally.

Device configuration updates – devices at the edge will need to be configured locally as services change. The edge could be able to manage this remotely.

Diagnostics of connected devices – the use of analytics at the edge can be used to identify specific problems with devices in the field through machine learning or pattern recognition.

Edge node or gateway management – device management platforms can be used to manage the operator's edge infrastructure as well as the IoT device.

Benefits of the Edge to this Use Case

Better control at the edge

Device management at the edge means that IoT devices are better controlled resulting in increased efficiency and improved quality of service. Where constraints are identified in edge computing, additional resources can be brought online to reduce problematic areas and better manage service scalability. Additionally, IoT services such as data access by third parties can be managed effectively if control is available at the edge node.

Better management of device performance

Enforced consistency of device configurations and performance criteria at the edge mean that there are fewer variables to contend with, which means in turn, that applications can be confidently optimised to obtain the best performance. Additionally, device performance data can be collected effectively at the edge for further analysis.

Effective deployment of applications at the edge

The use of a device management platform at the edge means that applications can be distributed to appropriate edge locations. If an IoT deployment has a number of different edges to manage, an application can be deployed to the edge closest to the device to obtain lowest latency, if a customer is paying for a premium service.

More efficient distribution of device updates

Distributing patches and firmware updates to devices is a key feature of a device management platform. Bringing edge infrastructure into the ecosystem means that these updates can be made more efficient as the edge can better manage local network resources for distribution to local devices.

Integrated hardware and software ecosystem

Device management that manages all aspects of the edge, including devices, applications and connectivity means that a single ecosystem can be created, where control is able to be exerted across all elements of an edge deployment. This means that the service can be optimised for different uses, enhancing quality of service as a result.

Design Considerations for Device Management at the Edge

Device management at the edge allows efficiencies of IoT deployments to be fully realised. By reducing the load on the cloud and its associated device management and analytics engines by moving processing to the edge, the system as a whole becomes more efficient.

- Support for device types

    The device ecosystem is very diverse and therefore management of devices at the edge must be tailored to support different types, classes and configurations of IoT device. Some of these devices will have more computing power than others and the device management platform will have to understand which devices can operate independently and which will rely more heavily on edge processing or require centralised management in the cloud.

Context awareness
: As IoT devices perform a wide range of functions at all times of day, the device management services at the edge will have to be aware of the device context- this means not applying updates at a time when an IoT device might be especially active, or in certain locations.

Multi-access edge computing
: Some edge devices will use multiple networks to communicate with the cloud (as per the ETSI Multi-access Edge Computing model2). This means that device management needs to be aware of which network a device is using and what data is being passed across it. This may affect configuration management if some updates can only be performed over certain networks.

Security

The IoT, by its very nature, is a distributed, complex network of devices. Edge computing pushes much of the logic and data storage for effective operation of the IoT closer to the end devices, and having security services also distributed at the edge offers the opportunity to improve security capabilities, as well as offering native security for new low latency applications.

The edge has an important role to play in data security. Many advanced tools and techniques can be applied to ensure that the edge contributes to the security of the overall IoT deployment. With a vast array of different equipment and devices connected to the IoT, security services at the edge can be used to comprehensively secure or even isolate complex industrial environments such as smart factories and buildings, as well as be used to ensure that data privacy is maintained in applications handling personal data such as CCTV or automated licence plate readers.

Security at the IoT edge should be treated the same as any other secure environment, but there are new tools that can be used to ensure security at new edge and device levels. For example, using strong identity management for devices at the edge means that authentication is more straight-forward, as does robust definition of edge processes to ensure that they remain secure.

A number of security issues can be addressed at the edge in an IoT environment:

Firmware and other updates
Secure update of firmware and other device updates from the edge using public key certification or secure transmissions such as SSL ensure that firmware upgrades are carried out securely.

Data Authentication
Authentication of data and updates at the edge is important to retain secure environments. Authentication is likely to be via a certificate-based system. Implementation of this will need careful consideration to prevent poor performance of edge processing and latency.

Access Control
Identity and permissions management at the edge is important to ensure that access to data at the edge is managed securely. Granting data access to third parties means that full access control policies must be in place.

Prevention of Denial of Service attacks
Analysis of the data flow from IoT devices to spot and prevent characteristics of DDoS attacks.

Benefits of the Edge to this Use Case

The distributed nature of edge computing for IoT means that malicious attacks aimed at the network are harder to instigate as attacking single nodes will only have limited impacts. The edge also offers more processing power to prevent attacks such as DDoS in addition to the central core.

The IoT edge offers a new way of securing IoT end-points which may not be running the most up-to-date firmware or operating system. Security services at the edge can be used to ensure that devices with a high risk profile can be more easily isolated or have their data actively intercepted and secured.

Data and device provenance – as processing and data storage moves closer to the edge, the origination point of data is better understood and can be recorded with greater confidence.

Processing of authentication, identity and access management – although sometimes constrained, additional processing power at the edge can be used for robust security processes as well as customer applications, meaning that security processes can be applied to ever increasing volumes of data.

Design Considerations

Using the edge environment to enhance IoT security could improve trust for the service being offered, but there are a number of considerations that should be considered in any deployment.

Constrained resources

Processing resources at the edge are constrained compared with centralised services, and so the same models for securing data and access at the edge may not be the most effective to apply at the edge – at the very least they will need to be re-configured to best make use of the resources available.

Appropriate policies
IoT at the edge must have relevant policies available that are applicable to both IoT and edge use cases. These policies must be applied whenever data access is granted or updates are to be sent to devices. Failure to implement robust policies will mean that attacks are more likely to succeed.

Minimise attack vectors
By focusing IoT activity at the edge through, for example, only selective data generation and collection, some attack vectors could be minimised. Holding and transporting less data makes the system more secure, and also frees up system resources for better security management and authentication. The location of data processing needs to be appropriate – there may be classes of IoT data which can only be analysed in the cloud or highly secured data centres, for example.

Priority Messaging

Much of the data generated by the IoT will be of low value – unexceptional status updates and low priority data. However, some data will be of great importance and needs to be prioritised to ensure it is acted upon rapidly. This 'critical data' is likely to be a very small percentage of the total volume generated, yet is the most important. The scope of priority messaging goes beyond just single applications, as these message types could be used to initiate a cascade of actions across different applications and devices.

Examples of priority messaging include:

Transportation - accident alert that needs to be sent to following vehicles to enable them to avoid collision.

Health & Safety - fire alarm linked to building evacuation.

Environmental - rainfall or pollution above maximum safe levels linked to remedial activities.

Security – unauthorised activity leading to automated security actions e.g. doors closing; terrorism response in immediate vicinity; drones flying into no-fly areas.

Industrial – failure of critical component requiring immediate shutdown of other systems; construction worker in unsafe location.

The edge enables high priority data needs to be generated, sent, processed, and actioned more quickly than sending the data to the cloud.

Design Considerations
Fast processing at the edge – low latency means that priority messages can be acted upon more quickly at the edge. Having relevant data storage and applications in a local cloudlet means that messages are received and acted upon quickly, without having to rely on centrally held data or applications.

Message association – devices do not need to operate in isolation at the edge, and a priority message from one device may well be replicated by another nearby, meaning that the scale of any issue can be quickly judged.

Routing – processing of priority messages at the edge means that their routing can be optimised through the rest of the network architecture, so they get to a specific endpoint in the fastest possible time.

Battery life – data prioritisation at the edge means that low powered IoT devices can save battery life and processing power by leaving the actioning of critical data to the edge node.

Design Considerations
Priority messaging will need to be considered as part of the overall design of IoT products, networks and data processing services. There are different types of priority messaging. Primarily, priority messages are in a known format as an output of a known process, for example, a fire alarm. Sometimes the message may not be identified as high priority by the device, but processing at the edge could still identify it as such. For example, voltage fluctuations in a smart grid may need the aggregation of data from different devices to determine priority.

High priority messaging and subsequent actions are enabled by the IoT edge. By only communicating with local IoT gateways and cloudlets, and keeping the impact of priority messaging local, faster responses can be assured. Data that has a wider impact beyond the immediate locale can be uploaded to the central cloud for further dissemination and decision making either immediately or after the local situation has been handled; for example, to feed in to larger datasets for analytics purposes.

For high priority messaging to be actioned quickly, near real-time processing of data is required. When tagged data is received, it can be easily identified and prioritised if the correct classifications are set-up within applications at the edge gateway. For other data, further processing could be used to identify data coming from multiple applications and devices to allow it to be prioritised in the same way.

The application on the edge node or gateway will need to make an automated decision as to what action to take with a high priority message. It may well be that a pre-defined process is initiated for known data types from known applications or devices. For example, a drone drifting into unauthorised areas can be redirected to a new flight path through a pre-defined process that all drones will need to recognise.

"By only communicating with local IoT gateways and cloudlets, and keeping the impact of priority messaging local, faster responses can be assured."

Data Replication

Many IoT services are not localised – they are spread across a large geographic area or devices need to move between different locations on the mobile network. To support low latency at the edge, some applications may need access to a localised data store at each location that they move to. This data store needs to be consistent across all instances of the application to ensure consistent results. This data may be time sensitive – a weather forecast, traffic conditions or distributed ledger instance, for example. Without access to this data locally, applications will need to query the cloud, which will affect latency and creates single points of dependency. By replicating data across multiple sites, this issue can be avoided, and a seamless experience created at every location.

Benefits of Edge for this Use Case

Replicated data has the following benefits:

- Efficiencies of IoT at the edge can be fully realised, across multiple locations. Not having to call to the cloud for master data significantly increases the performance of an application.
- Low latency support – by having local direct access to relevant data at the edge, low latency can be better realised.
- Disaster recovery - by distributing data across multiple locations, disaster recovery becomes possible, as data can be replicated across multiple locations, reducing the risk of data loss even if a node were to fail.
- Scalability - heavy processing of data can be distributed across all available processing

power, meaning that a system is not reliant on a single cloud or core source for transactional processing power. Distribution may be possible across different vendor systems with the correct standards in place.

Design Considerations for Replicated Data

There will generally be a need to have certain data ultimately held in the cloud for long-term storage, analytics and future processing. However, real-time data and logic that is needed for the operation of a wide variety of services under an IoT edge computing architecture must be available as an application needs it, without the latency implicit in storing and processing data centrally.

Time synchronisation

In order to synchronise data replicated across multiple locations, there will likely need to be time synchronisation at all edge locations. To ensure consistent data across multiple nodes, time must be accurate, otherwise data at different locations may not be fully synchronised.

Preventing task duplication

The use of distributed ledgers to store transactions at edge nodes is a good way to ensure consistency of data and messages across replicated nodes – once a message or task has been completed, this could be recorded in the ledger to ensure that the activity is replicated to every peer node.

Master data

Although distributed data is important for real-time transactions, a master data set is likely to be needed from a central location, to govern how the local instances should operate. Centralised operation of multiple cloudlets is needed to ensure that there is a distinct hierarchy in place for issue resolution and effective control of multiple systems.

Personal data

As data is replicated across nodes, special consideration should be given to personal data that would be affected by the EU GDPR and similar regulations. Data replication processes should have scope to identify personal data and the way that should be handled.

Node to node communication

If enabled, nodes are able to communicate with each other. This means a process of ensuring that data sets are replicated without reference to master data sources inside the cloud. Data must be replicated directly into other nodes where the local application may need access to up-to-date data.

Security

Data authentication at the edge requires local attributes to be held to ensure data is authenticated with low latency. Holding this information in the centralised cloud would slow down operations where authentication is needed.

Device management

Device configurations may need to be replicated across multiple nodes at the edge to ensure that any device management services are applied at the appropriate time or location.

Cloud Enablement

The edge is expected to be attractive to cloud vendors as it offers them the potential to better distribute data storage and processing power to support low latency services, support higher systems availability and also to reduce the load on their existing data centres. A mutually beneficial relationship between cloud providers and mobile operators should exist at the edge, where operators have local resources to enable IoT edge for cloud providers, and cloud providers have platforms suitable for enabling a wide range of services on the operator's edge infrastructure. Local infrastructure also meets customer and regulatory requirements about data storage on premises or in the country, if edge resources can be located in the relevant location. Some IoT users such as factories or smart cities may also insist on their data being stored and managed locally.

From a service point of view, IoT edge environments will rarely operate completely in isolation. A connection to a centralised cloud will often be required for control, monitoring and update purposes at the very least, and so the dynamic between the edge and cloud is a complex one. A hybrid edge and cloud architecture can offer the best of both worlds.

Built-in scalability

By enabling distributed resources, scalability of IoT services at the larger end of the scale becomes achievable. Even if resources at the edge are unable to cope with the scale of operations required by a deployment, there can be a fallback to the cloud, meaning that some or all of the service can be maintained.

Benefits of Edge for this Use Case

Linking the IoT edge and cloud has many benefits, across network, application and data management.

Maximise use of resources both locally and centrally

By linking the edge and the cloud, the most appropriate resources for specific tasks can be identified and allocated. This means efficient usage of resources in the operators domain, perhaps held at local base stations, or on the device itself, or in the cloud providers domain, where huge data volumes can be centrally stored.

Integrated view of data

Integrating the edge and cloud means that users will have a view over the status and location of all data relevant to their application or service. A seamless view means that the quality of service which can be achieved without having to resort.

Security

Full integration of edge and cloud means that data security can be overseen from a single source. Utilising the relevant cloud agents ensures that data can be securely transmitted across the cloud, edge and device.

Enablement of new business models

Business models including Infrastructure as a Service (IaaS) or higher response level Service Level Agreements enabled by lower latency can be introduced with integrated cloud and edge access. Unified billing for processing and storage can be managed across the cloud and edge in processes seamless to the end user. The edge can reside in different locations of the IoT deployment chain, and any cost benefits can be used to create new business models.

Design Considerations

Approach to data processing

A "Slow Lane" / "Fast Lane" approach is necessary to ensure that data is held in the correct location and processing resources are prioritised accordingly. "Fast Lane" data will obviously be dealt with first, and likely to be processed as fully at the edge as possible, for all the reasons stated elsewhere in this paper. "Slow Lane" data on the other hand is likely to be backhauled at an appropriate time to the cloud for processing. "Slow Lane" data may provide a more comprehensive view of what is occurring, but it will take time to achieve that view. To facilitate this model, appropriate data analytics models and data categorisation need to be put into place by the analytics provider.

Support for cloud agents

Many cloud providers have dedicated edge agents that will manage the relationship between the edge and the cloud. Recognition of these and integration of support for them into wider application and device management platforms will enable cloud integration for a wide range of service providers and encourage portability of applications.

Developer support

Developers commonly look to incorporate cloud support and functionality in their applications, and the same will be true of IoT applications at the edge. Access to the edge infrastructure and platforms should be implemented in the relevant tools to enable the developer community to take advantage of benefits edge offers the IoT.

> *"Integrating the edge and cloud means that users will have a view over the status and location of all data relevant to their application or service."*

IoT Solutions
IoT Image and Audio Processing

Devices such as cameras, including CCTV, and microphones can provide data for processing by IoT platforms and applications, such as licence plate reading or monitoring noise pollution. IoT edge introduces new ways of analysing this data without having to backhaul the entire image or audio stream. An edge cloudlet can be used to process the image, video or audio data to determine key information, such as licence plate numbers or the number of people in an area, meaning that only a small amount of data, such as the licence number itself is forwarded or stored. Other examples where the camera can be used as a sensor include for monitoring of environmental conditions such as river levels, monitoring crowd density, or in industrial IoT, whether on a factory floor, monitoring powerlines from a drone, or listening for flow through pipelines to identify leaks.

Benefits of Edge for this Use Case

Low cost

Cameras and microphones are relatively low cost to procure, install and maintain for the insights they can provide; use of edge processing means that network management costs are also managed effectively, making them an attractive general purpose alternative to dedicated IoT sensors.

Significant reduction in network backhaul

By identifying objects within images, without needing to send the image itself to upstream servers, the amount of data that needs to be transmitted back to the core is significantly reduced.

Quick decision making

Fast processing means that it is possible to support a wider range of real-time or near real-time applications – speeding up the management of production lines or enabling new ways of charging drivers at tollgates and so on.

More flexible IoT sensor arrays

By adding camera data to IoT deployments, a more comprehensive analysis can be taken, as cameras can add more general context (through both imaging of a location and broad image coverage) than many other types of IoT sensors.

Enabling new use cases

New IoT use cases become possible with the use of cameras and microphones as sensors. For example, the use of image processing for recognising yields, pests and diseases of crops whilst they grow.

Design Considerations

Design and deployment considerations for image and audio processing mainly focus on image and camera setup to ensure that the data source is good enough for analysis, but other considerations are also relevant.

Image or audio quality

Information can only be recognised from a camera image or audio stream if the quality is good enough – this means high enough resolution, but also the ability to recognise from an image or audio stream in all environmental conditions – day and night, sun and rain, crowd/ traffic. If this is not possible, the analytics will not be fit for purpose.

Image & audio format

Images can be still or video and along with audio can come in a variety of formats and obtained using a variety of standard and proprietary protocols. Analytics engines will need the image data to be decoded to frame data. Video images may need to be broken down into a series of still images for analysis. Collected data will ideally be in a common, open format so that it can be managed by a range of analytics engines.

Data analytics

A picture is worth a thousand words, but for IoT analytics purposes, there needs to be a very clear definition of the parameters that are needed from an image or audio file, so that machine learning processes can be trained. This means that a clear definition of the image topography or audio landscape and how it relates to the data to be extracted must be defined in advance.

Camera setup

In some cases, it may be simpler if the camera is in a fixed position with a number of reference points that do not change, so that the image processing engine can accurately identify the area of the image to process.

Operator Opportunity

IoT Foundation

The edge is a natural evolution of today's IoT architecture deployed by mobile operators. Evolution of platforms, processes and propositions will enable operators to introduce edge seamlessly into their foundational IoT services, such as connectivity and device management, whilst retaining the attributes which they are renowned for – connectivity, security and scalability.

The edge offers new ways of creating efficient connectivity services specifically designed to benefit IoT deployments by reducing the amount of data which is backhauled to the cloud. Better options for managing devices in the field become available, with distributed management of firmware updates and applications possible. IoT platforms will need to extend their reach to the edge, and operators will be in a strong position to ensure that network, security and cloud services are integrated effectively at the edge.

IoT Service Enablers

Data Management at the edge will be crucial for operators in ensuring quality of service and effective analytics of IoT data. Managing customer data in a secure fashion and ensuring a seamless integration between user, cloud, application, edge and device will allow a new generation of service offerings from operators.

IoT devices can benefit greatly from local processing power, data management and analytics. Having the ability to prioritise messages and manage the large volume of data from massive IoT deployments means that operators can both maximise the cost savings on their own network, but pass on better service levels to their customers.

There is a mutually beneficial relationship with cloud providers that operators can also build through a combination of local infrastructure controlled by the operator and the data management platforms from cloud providers, to enable a new generation of IoT management services.

IoT Solutions

The edge offers operators both opportunities for new IoT solutions and new ways of managing existing services. IoT sensors which generate large amounts of data such as cameras can be used to provide new or better insights, and data from multiple sensors can be combined to create new levels of analysis.

Advanced IoT solutions such as support for V2X communications or smart factories can benefit from these new opportunities that operators can introduce. By making the edge the standard place for managing applications and services, new levels of service management, automation and precision can be achieved.

Potential Next Steps

Deployment of IoT edge and applications that will utilise it is not a trivial task, and there are a number of challenges that will need to be addressed. Operators will need to strike a balance between the benefits that edge brings in scaling and managing IoT deployments and the costs of setting up a service. A number of potential next steps for the industry have been identified:

Common Framework

- Define end user requirements for customers and application developers.
- Define where the IoT edge resides for defined use cases – at the cloudlet in the data centre, on the base station, or closer to the device.
- Understand deployment and business models and match to the infrastructure that could be utilised.

Evaluate Solutions

- Evaluate different edge models, consortiums and technologies for their suitability to IoT deployments.
- Understand the need for IoT platform extensions at the edge, and how the functionality available maps to IoT use cases.

Operator Roles

- Understand the roles of different partners through the value chain and how the operator can create value for them.

Understand cloud offerings at the edge and how the operator can integrate with them or support them. Engage with cloud providers to create a mutually beneficial model for deployment of edge services from both the operators and cloud providers.

- Undertake relevant pilots and other activities to investigate the benefits of edge for

IoT customers.

Chapter 6.
Standards and Role of open source

This chapter describes the standardization/open source activities required to support the previously identified needed services and capabilities.

Standards for self-organization, self-configuration, self-discovery

There is no doubt that with the growth in the number of ECNs, the management of the network, the ECN and the application will become a huge challenge. To facilitate the deployment of ECNs, it is better to mask the complexity of the technology from operators and users, and to realize the plug and play of devices. Therefore, it is necessary to introduce autonomic networking. Currently, the autonomous functions already exist. However, the discovery, node identification, negotiation, transport, messaging and security mechanisms, as well as non-autonomic management interfaces, are being realized separately. This isolation of functions is leading to high OpEx.

Engineering Task Force (IETF) is developing a system of autonomic functions to manage the network at a higher level without detailed low-level management of individual devices. In a secure closed-loop interaction mechanism, the network elements cooperate to satisfy management intent: network processes coordinate their decisions and translate them into local actions.

In the cellular communication domain, 3GPP has proposed the self-organizing network (SON), aimed at making the planning, configuration, management, optimization and healing of mobile radio access networks simpler and faster. Since Release 8, 3GPP has begun the research and standardization of SON, the motivation being to deal with more parameters in network configuration, more complex network structures and the coexistence of the 2G/3G/LTE network. Newly added base stations should be self-configured to realize the plug and play. Moreover, based on network performance and radio conditions, the base station will self-optimize its parameters and behaviour. When outage occurs, the self-healing will be triggered to temporarily compensate the performance loss before a permanent solution is found.

Standards which allow low OpEX management of ECN and software will also be self organized as well.

Trust/ decentralized trust

The ISO/IEC 15408 Standard defines trust as "a calculation configuration in which components, operations or processes involved in the calculation are predictable under any condition and are resistant to viruses and physical disturbances".

Trust in this sense means that the services provided by the computer system can be proved to be trustworthy. In other words, the services provided are trustworthy from the user's point of view and this trustworthiness is provable.

Trust computing as defined by the Trust Computing Group (TCG) has the following meaning:

§ User authentication: the trust of the user
§ Platform hardware and software configuration correctness: the user's trust in the platform environment
§ The integrity and legitimacy of the application: the trust in the application running
§ Verifiability between platforms: the mutual trust between the platforms in the network

The decentralization trend is driven by the distributed system; for instance, an edge computing system, in which no central hub acts, so a new approach to security and trust are needed based on the distributed architecture.

There exists a general view that the blockchain's distributed architecture offers a valid framework for tackling distributed system security and trust challenges. The blockchain is a distributed database that maintains a continuously growing list of records, called blocks, secured from tampering and revision. Each block contains a timestamp and a link to a previous block. By design, blockchains are inherently resistant to modification of the data – once recorded, the data in a block cannot be altered retroactively.

ISO Technical Committee 307 is now dedicated to standardization of blockchains and distributed ledger technologies to support secure and trust interoperability and data interchange among users, applications and systems.

Credible information

Credible information is crucial for an edge computing system. Credibility of information depends on trust in the system which generates the information. Trust is defined to be "confidence that an operation, data transaction source, network or software process can be relied upon to behave as expected" in IEC 62443-3-3 [63]. IEC 62443-3-3 describes system security requirements for industrial automation and control systems (IACS), and it currently does not list trust as a requirement explicitly. Even though security implies a guarantee of trust, it can be useful to review whether some additional system requirements, e.g. requirements on system integration and operation, are necessary to realize trust in IACS. It can also be beneficial to investigate what additional requirements are necessary when dealing with trust in horizontal edge computing systems.

E/W communication Standards between multiple ECNs

There are several layers of E/W communication in question:

1) Physical layer: A number of Standards exist for mesh networking via physical layer relay and any of these can/could be used. It might be worth considering how that mesh might be implemented efficiently in wired networks, and also whether the physical radio Standards might be merged with the narrowband IoT protocols for long-range operation.

2) Link layer protocols: Here again, numerous protocols exist (IEEE 802.1aq in wired, and IEEE 802.15.4-ZigBee [64] or Z-Wave [65] and WIA-PA in wireless). Again, a merge with narrowband IoT protocols should be considered to allow mesh operation in narrowband IoT for long range operation.

3) In the autonomous control domain, time-sensitive data must be transmitted within strict bounds of latency and reliability. In the case that E/W-bound communication is required between ECNs in industrial automation, automotive or robotic environments, TSN may be needed to prioritize time-sensitive traffic in crowded networks. TSN is currently under development within IEEE 802.1 and the Deterministic Networking working group of IETF.

4) Data layer: A flexible data ontology, allowing common definition of data types and meanings across the network. This is an area where both Standards bodies and open source may play a role, such as one M2M and OPC-UA.

The majority of open source work might be concentrated in the area of high level data processing in the mesh by elaborating on existing, proven and recommended Standards (such as MQTT) within an open reference architecture. For example, an overarching reference architecture could employ a lightweight MQTT implementation to accept not only north/south (N/S) but also E/W transactions between modules. This could be implemented as a single queue (all transactions E/W, N/S) or as two queues, one operating for E/W and another for N/S. It can be noted that in the items above, a mesh can be implemented at each layer, but it is only with the inclusion of item 3) that an application level E/W communication can be achieved.

Finally, successful implementation of E/W communication depends on implementation of decentralized trust.

Containerization Standard for embedded systems

Linux containers, Docker for example, offer for the first time a practical path to using virtualization on embedded devices, as the latter do not require a very complex hypervisor architecture to operate. Containerization of IoT applications, particularly at the ECN level, would be greatly facilitated by the creation of a common Standard for virtualisation support on IoT nodes. This would be an expansion of the ground covered by OCI [60], which has initiated a general effort.

There are a number of challenges facing an implementation:

§ The extreme heterogeneity of device type
§ Severely restricted resource envelopes in terms of storage, CPU, and networking
§ Devices that are difficult to reach or re-provision upon failure, where power is unstable and may be turned off at any time, or which have custom hardware attached, requiring deep version interoperability, i.e. when the device returns online after weeks or months, an upgrade to the container can be made spanning several versions.

Open standard for implementation of algorithm for machine learning

As discussed earlier, the complexity of CNNs, HMMs, natural language processing and other disciplines used in the creation of ML algorithms and DNNs requires storage and computing resources. Clearly the backend processing in embedded devices is currently an open source initiative, and since it has started in this manner, it is likely to remain so, with Caffe and a few others becoming de facto Standards.

To implement ML upon lower powered, cheaper, embedded devices, it would seem to be a reasonable approach to implement a specific hardware-based method of accepting the introduced ML models and then acting upon them, i.e. comparing the models with incoming live data.

Already some efforts have been made in this area; for example, the recent Intel Quark implementation of comparison functions [59]. These efforts are proprietary and no Standards have been defined to cover the loading and comparison of features.

If Standards were defined in the loading of models and comparison of data, it would provide the greatest degree of interoperability between different offerings from different processor manufacturers.

Comprehensive standard tackling carrier mode selection in case of loss of connectivity
Connectivity is offered by many providers of mobile and Wi-Fi networks. Some even have global coverage or globally scattered coverage; for example, iPass, a network of Wi-Fi access points across the globe, or Eduroam that has Wi-Fi access points across universities.

Currently, human users can select the network and input the credentials. Some locations, e.g. hotels, offer a QR code for the credentials.

In case the connection is lost, the human has to intervene and connect to a new network. For IoT or safety and security use cases, this interaction is not possible or even productive. There are Standards for sending recommendations regarding which networks to use, with associated policies; for example, Open Mobile Alliance (OMA) Device Management, based on HTTP. The Standard was adopted by 3GPP on the interface between the UE and the ANDSF network component. It supports recommended network policies depending on the time of the day, the location and the prioritized networks to be connected. The UE can thus connect independently to a new network when connectivity is lost. Unfortunately, the policy does not include the very important aspect of price. Being a Standard oriented to the telecommunications industry, it did not reach out to the outside community.

For tackling IoT use cases, OMA has defined a new protocol, OMA Lightweight M2M that uses a more energy-efficient transport based on UDP. Its connectivity management policies are developing and it might have a broader impact on providing connectivity without human interaction.

Even so, there is a tremendous need across the vertical sectors to have a comprehensive standard tackling carrier mode selection, according to the connectivity modules built on the end device, be it Wi-Fi, 3G, LTE, soon 5G or any other type of access network.

Role of open source

Cloud computing has immensely benefitted from open sources such as Linux, Docker containers, Kafka messaging, Spark streaming and multi-tier storage. The result has been a highly scalable and standardized infrastructure that meets computational and lifecycle management demands and provides a common environment for developers, driving down the cost of software solutions.

The need for standardization and open source for the edge is even greater. The edge is where vendor-specific solutions need to interoperate. Without this interoperation, IoT cannot fulfil its promises.

As discussed earlier, microservices or pods need to be deployed on the edge (devices, IoT gateways, micro data centre, etc.) as well as in the cloud, so that applications can be configured in an optimal way, e.g. to address huge data volumes, real-time requirements and variances in connectivity.

As history has shown, open source projects fulfil these needs better than standardization of interfaces and architectures.

Companies providing solutions in edge computing will have plenty of room for differentiation and revenue generation by providing differentiating functionalities, domain specific solutions, better services, higher QoS, etc.

At the time of the writing of this White Paper, the Linux Foundation project Edge X Foundry appears to be a candidate to address a common edge computing platform.

Chapter 7.
Introduction to Edge Computing in IIoT

Almost every use case and every connected device focused on by the Industrial Internet Consortium (IIC) requires some sort of compute capability at its source, at the edge. Multiple sources define edge computing as "cloud computing systems that perform data processing at the edge of the network, near the source of the data". While this is certainly true, it only scratches the surface of the immense power and remarkable capabilities that edge computing applications and architectures can provide to solve industrial internet users' toughest challenges. But, as is typical with any powerful technology, innovative architectures and new terminology are needed to facilitate implementation, bringing increased complexity with it.

This chapter provides practical guidance on edge computing, architectures and the building blocks necessary for an edge computing implementation. It defines edge computing architectural functions and highlights key use case considerations.

Consequently, there is a need to identify:
- where the edge is,
- its defining characteristics,
- key drivers for implementing edge computing and
- why compute capabilities should be deployed at the edge in Industrial Internet of Things (IIoT) systems.

It also informs architecture and testbed teams through:
- identifying and evaluating standards, practices and characteristics best suited for addressing edge computing holistically, and highlighting gaps where needed,
- identifying deployment models and crosscutting functions that address patterns and characteristics for edge computing deployment and
- exploring and identifying extensions to the current edge computing model that expand and enhance the functionality of edge computing devices.

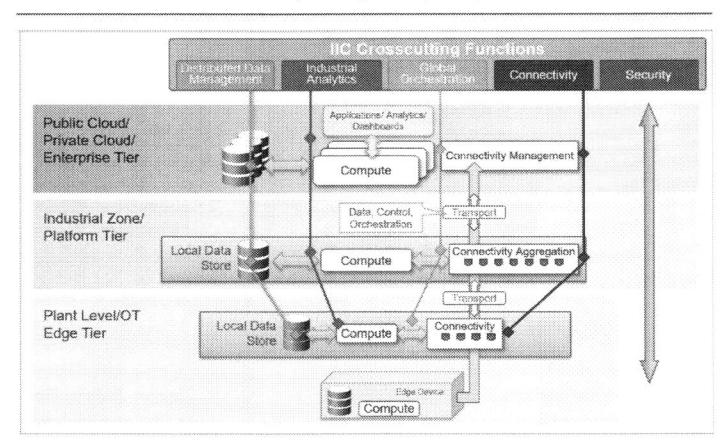

Figure 7.1: IIoT Architectures

Where is the Edge?

The edge is a logical layer rather than a specific physical divide, so it is open to individual opinion and interpretation of "where" the edge is. The business and usage viewpoints provide clues, while the functional and implementation viewpoints deal with the technical aspects.

From the business perspective, the location of the edge depends on the business problem or "key objectives" to be addressed.

"Key objectives are quantifiable high-level technical and ultimately business Quote outcomes expected of the resultant system…" and "Fundamental capabilities refer to high-level specifications of the essential ability of the system to complete specific major business tasks" (Ref IIRA).

There is a continuum of fundamental capabilities for an IIoT solution and "the edge" moves along this continuum based on the requirements of the problem at hand, as shown by the following examples found in typical industrial operations.

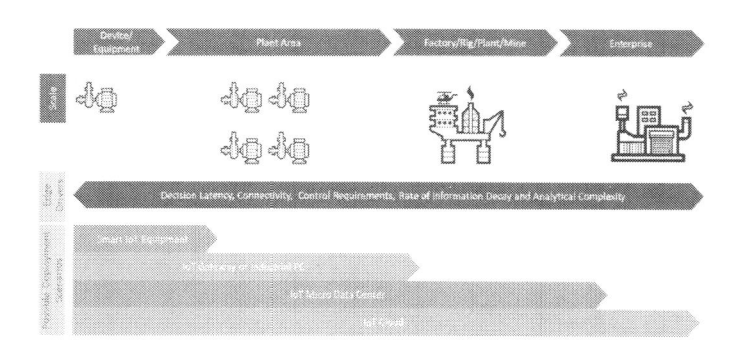

Figure 7.2: Edge Layers

EXAMPLE 1: MONITOR THE PERFORMANCE OF PLANT AREAS OR PRODUCTION LINES

The performance of equipment and production lines are often expressed through performance indicators like Overall Equipment Effectiveness (OEE). Near real-time analytics on multiple data points from sensors in the plant area can be processed on a local gateway and provide OEE trends and alerts to operational systems or personnel. In this case, the fundamental capability requires information from multiple equipment sources to perform simple analytics. The time value of information is high as response delays waiting for decisions from the cloud can cause significant losses. This business problem suggests that the edge is at the plant area level.

EXAMPLE 2: OPTIMIZE SUPPLY CHAIN FOR A LOCATION OR FACTORY TWICE DAILY

Optimizing supply chain processes for a local facility, factory or an oil field requires data from multiple sources at short intervals to apply optimization algorithms and analytics that will adapt supply-chain plans in business systems such as SCM or ERP. The fundamental capability requires local or factory-level connectivity with decisions made in hours. Additional information outside the perimeter of the factory may be useful, but not mandatory for effective optimization. In this instance, the edge is at the perimeter of the factory, plant or local facility.

EXAMPLE 3: PREDICT EQUIPMENT FAILURE AND SCHEDULE PROACTIVE RESPONSE

Machine learning models to predict Electric Submersible Pump (ESP) failures require data from multiple offshore platforms. The analytics models are complex and a large amount of data is needed to train and re-train the models. It also requires regular data feeds from operating ESPs to determine each unit's remaining useful life. The data from individual ESPs need to be analysed regularly but information decay is much slower than in the other scenarios and decisions can be taken daily or weekly. Computation is typically performed at the enterprise level using a public or private cloud and is at the top end of the edge continuum.

The edge can be anywhere along the time-value graph (see Figure 7.3) as these examples illustrate.

It is "where" data for sensors is used to achieve a specific key objective or address a specific business problem.

Why Compute at the Edge

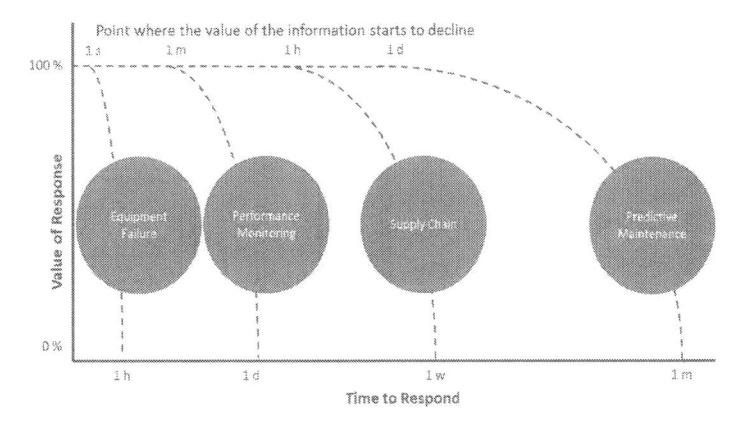

Figure 7.3: Time-Value Graph

Edge computing is a decentralized computing infrastructure in which computing resources and application services can be distributed along the communication path from the data source to the cloud. That is, computational needs can be satisfied "at the edge," where the data is collected, or where the user performs certain actions. The benefits are:

- improved performance,
- compliance, data privacy and data security concerns are satisfied and
- reduced operational cost.

We examine each in turn.

IMPROVE PERFORMANCE

Improve Performance	Compliance, Privacy, Security	Reduce Operational Cost
Alerts, analytics and applications run faster close to the originating source of data	Leverage local computing based in a specific area, region or domain of the required compliance, privacy or security boundaries	Reduce connectivity, data migration and bandwidth costs associated with sending data to the cloud
Improved robustness, reliability and local processing enables Autonomous execution of processes, rules and algorithms	Transferring data by definition exposes data to security threats as does storage in shared data centers	Analyzing and filtering data at the Edge reduces communication costs, cloud processing and cloud storage
Increase resiliency and uptime by eliminating round trips to data center	Protect privacy by anonymizing and analyzing data close to the source	

The edge is not merely a way to collect data for transmission to the cloud, it also processes, analyses and acts on the collected data at the edge within milliseconds and is therefore essential for optimizing industrial data at every aspect of an operation.

In a windfarm, for example, if wind speed or direction changes, the edge software onsite can analyse this data in real-time and adjust individual turbines to optimize overall wind farm production. Only aggregated data is sent to the cloud, reducing communication bandwidth requirements and improving data transfer time.

In addition, the turbines generate terabytes of data. Sending this data to a cloud platform to run advanced analytics may be technologically achievable, but cost prohibitive to do daily. Through edge computing, the end user can capture streaming data from a turbine and use it in real-time to prevent unplanned downtime and extend the life of the equipment while reducing the data set to a more manageable size for transmission to the cloud.

The challenge of transmitting large quantities of data in real-time cost-effectively from remote industrial sites can be mitigated by adding intelligence to devices at the edge of the network, in the plant or field. Edge computing on the device brings analytics capabilities closer to the machine and provides a less expensive option for optimizing asset performance.

COMPLIANCE, DATA PRIVACY AND DATA SECURITY

Public cloud creates a long list of privacy, regulatory and compliance issues related to classified or sensitive data. Today, service providers can guarantee private access and control but at the price of being cumbersome, costly, inelastic and difficult to manage.

Edge computing allows enterprises to operate independently using a public/private cloud by using local computing based in that area, region, domain or the required local security boundaries.

REDUCE OPERATIONAL COST

Connectivity, data migration, bandwidth and latency features of cloud computing are expensive. Edge computing addresses these by reducing bandwidth requirements and latency.

If an oil and gas company drilling in Nigeria, for example, requires computing to predict oil-well production-decline rate, the alternatives are to build their own data centres (with the associated cost and scale limitations) or to use a cloud provider (where the nearest datacentre can be 5,000 miles away) with significant costs and unreliable service. With edge computing, the end user can process data in real time locally at a fraction of the cost of the public cloud, while still maintaining the flexibility that a cloud infrastructure provides.

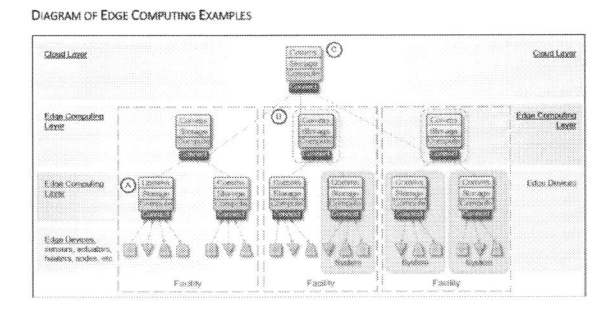

Figure 7.4: Cloud Infrastructure

Edge computing creates a valuable continuum from the device to the cloud to handle the massive amounts of data generated from IIoT. Processing data closer to where it is produced and at the response times required by the local applications addresses the challenges of rapidly increasing data volume. Edge computing decreases response time to events by eliminating a round trip to the cloud for analysis. It avoids costly bandwidth additions by eliminating the need to transmit gigabytes of data to the cloud. It also protects sensitive IIoT data by analysing it locally within a private network.

Consequently, enterprises using edge computing may improve and optimize operational performance, and address compliance and security concerns while efficiently managing costs.

The examples progress from left to right as the edge layer becomes more complex and aggregates multiple system functions below. The computing layer moves up the architecture stack, aggregating processing capabilities, information and data from below.

The multitude of choices means there is a layered edge-cloud synergy, rather edge versus cloud. Where possible, digitalization is always going to use edge and cloud synergistically in which fast and localized compute take place at the edge while global compute, model development, management and security can benefit from the "wisdom of the cloud".

Starting with an example of a simple temperature controller, the problem to be solved is temperature monitoring and control of a specific device or zone. In this case, the edge devices would be the thermocouple sending temperature data and the element providing the heating or cooling, and the edge computing device would be the temperature controller running the control algorithm and making the adjustments.

If the objective is to orchestrate temperature across several devices or areas, then the edge becomes the temperature controllers themselves (whether individual components or standalone systems) and the edge-computing layer becomes the system coordinating the control, typically a PLC or SCADA system ("B" in Figure 5).

If the business objective is to monitor and manage multiple geographically dispersed facilities, then the edge is each individual facility reporting its status to a compute layer in the cloud ("C" in Figure 5).

Characteristics of the IIoT Edge Computing Model

Edge computing exists vertically within the full stack from device to cloud and horizontally across IIoT subsystems. The new computing model is fully distributed and can support a wide range of interactions and communication paradigms including:

- peer-to-peer networking; for example, security cameras communicating about objects within their scope,
- edge-device collaboration such as self-organizing vehicles that travel together or a community of wind turbines in remote locations,
- distributed queries across data stored in devices, in the cloud and anywhere in between,
- distributed data management, defining where and what data is to be stored, and for how long and
- data governance including quality, discovery, usability, privacy and security aspects of data.

Key Drivers: Cloud to Edge Computing

IIoT disrupts the cloud-computing model with new usage scenarios leading to these requirements:

Time sensitive: Often decisions need to be made within milliseconds while a round trip to the cloud introduces undesirable latency. Reliability and critical-path control management make it too risky to rely solely on remote logic. A good example is autonomous guided vehicles; although an anti-collision algorithm can execute in the cloud, it is best to run the algorithms at the edge.

Communication: Mobile network infrastructure tends to follow the pattern of deploying to highly populated urban areas, before trickling down to rural or remote locations. For assets that are truly remote, satellite connectivity may be the only option. This creates a paradigm where IIoT use cases for industries such as mining, oil & gas, chemicals and shipping are not well served by robust affordable communication.

Data boundary: In some applications, the data produced and consumed by devices is required by other devices only within the local area. This local data can be acquired and served with low latency by the edge to the users in the local area. Depending upon the use case, the radius of the local area can vary from a few centimetres from the device to an entire neighbourhood or city. In augmented-reality scenarios, for example in smart cities, local edge infrastructures can store information about points of interest of a neighbourhood. Since most of the access to the data (or consumption of the data) will be made in the same local area, there is no need to store all information in the cloud. As a truck transitions from private to public network and across sovereign boundaries, both enterprise policies and local data regulation will determine what can be stored locally and what can be sent to the cloud.

Data volume: The amount of data generated by sensors can be huge. For example, hundreds of high-resolution cameras creating video streams at 30 frames per second could clog communication channels. Edge computing allows data to be processed and stored locally with only pre-processed data being transferred to the cloud.

IT/OT convergence: Historically the operational technologies (OT) that are used to manage and automate industrial equipment exist at the edge of the network while information technologies (IT) have been more centralized. Though these systems have been treated separately, there is value in having an integrated IT/OT strategy that offers:

• business data needed for interpreting or contextualizing IoT data for decision making,
• availability of both existing and new business outcomes, business models that leverage integrated data and
• standard processes to drive outcomes.

Data governance deals with quality, discovery, usability, privacy and security aspects of data. Insufficient data governance can leave a company vulnerable to major business disruptions. On the other hand, extreme data governance can stifle innovation. Edge computing helps simplify data governance by:

• reducing data clutter: high volume time-series data can be analysed at the edge,
• refining data usability: edge computing allows data to be contextualized resulting in better usability,
• improving data privacy: security policy at the edge allows only relevant data shared with the systems up in the hierarchy and
• lowering the impact of security breach: since edge computing allows for the data storage and analysis to be federated, impact of a security breach can be contained.

Use Cases

This section describes use cases that illustrate the benefits of edge computing. Figure 6 shows logical entities residing on either the cloud or the edge, connected through WANs. When clouds were first introduced, the trend was to "shift everything into the cloud", but, due to network latency and the cost to transmit a large amount of data, more logical tasks remained at the edge. With the improvement of the processing power and capability, the amount of tasks performed on the edge will continue to grow.

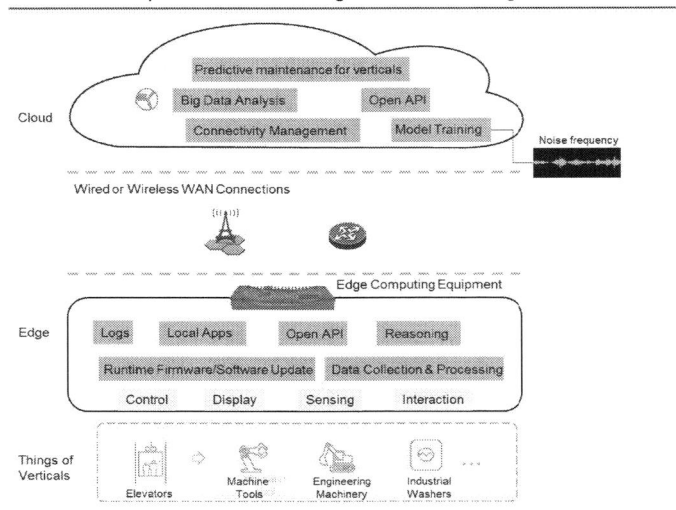

Figure 7.5: Logical Architecture Diagram for Edge Computing

To facilitate discussions on the boundaries and the necessary means to enable edge computing, there are "Key Requirements", "Edge Boundary" and "Edge Devices" clauses added to each use case. "Key Requirements" are not intended to be a standard so they are not normative. The "Edge Boundary" is one view from the contributor to the use case and is not intended to be definitive as typically, the boundary of each service or application varies as drawn by the system designers.

Similarly, the term "Boundary Devices" portrayed in the use cases by the contributors is not an exhaustive list.

Through the examination of all the use cases described here, we inferred general requirements for edge computing that may be common to all use cases:

Communications: Edge devices must continue to function even though data communications may be temporarily interrupted.

Edge device capability: The edge devices need to support edge-computing capabilities: communication, local computing and local storage.

Edge device functionality: The edge devices can be customized with features to fit various vertical industries, such as compact size, low power consumption, anti-vibration, electromagnetic shielding, waterproof and dust proof.

CREW SAFETY MANAGEMENT

Objective: Use wearable multi-gas detectors to monitor employees' exposure to harmful gases during a shift. Create real-time exposure profiles using data from the sensors and adjust the work schedule or work flow to prevent health issues.

Description of the use case: Safety in a hazardous or life-threatening operating environment, such as a mine, is a top issue. Other issues are production related, such as the status of the tools used, the status of the conveyer or vehicles used to carry out the ore, and the amount of ore produced in a measured period.

Key Requirements:

1. (Environment monitoring) poisonous gas detection, ambient temperature detection and control and lighting control need to be implemented.

2. (Personal monitoring) the personal vital-sign monitoring system must be installed locally and the data sent out to a central monitoring station in the operation centre.

Edge Boundary: Operation site (e.g. at the mine operation office or operation centre).

Edge Devices: Personal vital sign monitor (body temperature, heart rate and blood pressure, CO_2 level), personal tracker, environment monitors (ambient temperature, CO level, hazardous gas detection, lighting), tools, trucks and unmanned vehicles, conveyer belts and weighting devices.

FLEET TRACKING AND PLATOONING

Objective: Combine real-time GPS data with vehicle usage data from sensors to monitor and optimize the location and status of the fleet.

Description of the use case: A trucking company must operate its vehicles safely and efficiently. In addition to optimal routing in the delivery routes, the mechanical status of each vehicle can contribute to timely maintenance to improve the operation efficiency and safety. The operation is originally designed for individual trucks, but it can be extended to several trucks to form a "platoon" of unmanned trucks to increase operational efficiency.

Platooning is typically used for self-driving vehicles. The lead vehicle detects the lane and traffic condition to decide the optimal speed to manoeuvre. This information is then communicated through the following vehicles in the platoon. Each car has vehicle-to-vehicle (V2V) communication capabilities and controls for driving safety. The lead vehicle gathers the information, such as the location of the fleet and the operating condition of each vehicle, and reports to the office.

Key Requirements:

1. GPS based vehicle tracking supported by a local map.

2. The vehicle status monitoring system is installed locally, and the data shall be sent out to a central monitoring station in the operation centre.

3. A connection to a central location providing traffic updates

Edge Boundary: The lead vehicle of the platoon.

Edge Devices: Vehicle status monitor (engine speed, temperature, break pad thickness and hydraulic subsystem, transmission subsystem, weight and shock status, tire pressure, fuel level, etc.), GPS tracker, environment monitors (ambient temperature, lane detection, vicinity vehicle detection), container status monitor (for refrigerating) and V2V driving safety devices.

PREDICTIVE MAINTENANCE—CONNECTED ELEVATORS

Objective: With edge applications installed on connected elevators, operators and technicians are able to perform predictive maintenance of the elevators based on the data they provide at the edge.

Description of the use case: Operators of connected elevators rely on edge functions to achieve predictive maintenance of their systems for the systems to become more reliable and reduce system downtime. The operational cost of these systems is greatly reduced since the efficiency of the system can be significantly improved.

A connected elevator uses many sensors for gathering data on noise, vibration, temperature, etc. The operational status of the elevator can then be derived from analysing the sensed data. With elevators connected to edge computing devices, and the sensed data uploaded to the cloud, elevator operators can obtain the running status of all of their elevators. Elevator technicians are then able to perform predictive maintenance using edge computing data, and data in the cloud, to check and maintain those elevators selectively that are more likely to fail based upon analytics. Predictive maintenance increases the operational efficiency of the equipment while reducing the maintenance expense through targeted failure prevention and avoidance of unplanned downtime.

Key Requirements:

1. The edge devices offer containers, open APIs that allow third parties to develop applications to be installed on the edge devices.

2. To support 7 x 24 monitoring, the edge devices support runtime update of its software and firmware.

Edge Boundary: The elevator operations centre or the elevator itself

Edge Devices: Infrared sensors, weight sensors, smoke detectors, vibration inductors, noise sensors, cameras and operator interfaces.

Objective: Regulations in the food industry (e.g., EC 128/2002) require manufacturers to establish systems that enable traceability of food products across all stages of production, processing and distribution. While this use case focuses on the food industry, product traceability is important across multiple industries.

Description of the use case: Pieces of plastic in chocolate bars, bacterial contamination of cream cheese, falsely declared ingredients in pasta-based ready meals—a food product may be recalled for any number of reasons. Time is of the essence when it comes to product recalls. As well as damaging the manufacturer's reputation, these situations can be expensive, with costs rising as the whereabouts of the end products become less clear.

Bar codes, 2D codes, or electronic transponders are used to identify objects depending on whether they are individual items, primary and secondary packaging, pallets, trucks or containers. When it comes to deciding which technology to use, financial factors and the objects and processes involved must be taken into account. For example, a bar code can be printed onto an egg, while the cartons holding six or twelve eggs can be labelled with 2D codes and additional plain text such as the best-before date. A transponder, on the other hand, can be added to shipping cartons, pallets and other aggregated containers. The various methods of product identification described above ensure that the flow of materials across the supply chain are labelled, identified and tracked.

Industrial machinery, automated guided vehicles (AGVs) and collaborative robots or "cobots" are increasingly prevalent on the factory floor. The most targeted applications are packaging and palletizing, pick and place, machine tending and assembly and quality inspection. As issues may occur at any step in the supply chain including the quality or handling of materials, contamination introduced by people or machines or faulty processes, product quality and product traceability require orchestrating, recording and verifying the people, processes and machines involved.

Sensors with edge-computing capabilities allow these product identification methods to be checked against stored data for verification to ensure the flow of goods, people, process and machines. The right product goes into the right package and onto the shelf with critical information appearing correctly on the package and full genealogy available in the cloud.

Key Requirements:

1. Consider ambient conditions when selecting edge devices within the food industry, such as humidity, cold storage and outdoors.

2. Location and tracking of items across all stages of production, processing and distribution is important.

3. Sensors and computer vision systems identify particulates or contaminants in food.

4. Sensors and edge computing to orchestrate, record and verify the people, processes and machines involved.

Edge Computing and Industrial Analytics

Analytics is broadly defined as a discipline transforming data into information and business value through systematic analysis. Industrial analytics is the use of analytics in IIoT systems.

Advanced analytics is at the core of this next-generation level of transformation and, when applied to machine, process and grid data, provides new insights and intelligence to optimize decision-making and enable intelligent operations leading to transformational business outcomes and social value. These new insights and intelligence can be applied across any level of any industry if the appropriate data can be collected and analytics applied correctly. Some say data is the new oil. If that's the case, then data analytics is the new engine that propels the IIoT transformation.

Analytics can be classified in a number of different ways depending on where they are performed, the window of time for a relevant and meaningful response, and what functionality they are trying to achieve. A single analytical flow could involve edge analytics for initial distillation of data and immediate actuation, analytics in the cloud comingling the latest news from the edge with historic big data stores and back to the edge for further actuation.

TECHNOLOGY AND THE EVOLUTION OF INDUSTRIAL ANALYTICS

Advances in IT and OT capabilities such as compute capacity, communication bandwidth, low latency, software capability and sensor technology have removed technological constraints and allowed analytics to be deployed through an entire IoT system. For instance, looking at the edge tier of a system, the processing capability available at the edge in conjunction with low-latency communication have enabled algorithms to be run in real time supporting models that generate insights and real-time control for the system. Similarly, looking at the cloud tier, what was once impractical, performing streaming analytics on enormous data sets, is now possible thanks to big data compute capabilities and high-bandwidth communications. These same advances have also enabled the distribution of analytics so that they need not be centralized and can be implemented across the IIoT ecosystem.

WHERE SHOULD THE ANALYTICS BE PERFORMED?

Most industrial analytics deployments use a hybrid approach where analytics run at all tiers from edge to cloud, with analytics at a particular tier addressing a specific business objective.

Cost benefits stem from reducing the amount of data being sent to and stored in the cloud. Edge analytics mitigates the cost of storing and processing low-value and oft-repeated data. Analytical models are not helped by data noise. Instead of creating an unnecessary noisy big data problem, edge analytics can distil data prior to sending it on to the cloud.

Security Considerations for Edge Computing

Security is an important consideration for edge computing. More components and communication channels create a greater potential for attack vectors. Innovations are required to monitor, manage and secure globally distributed systems and contain inevitable breaches. The IISF documents a generalized end-to-end security framework. In edge computing implementations:

- security must be built-in to each device and at every level of the architecture,
- computing and networking endpoints must be monitored and managed,
- latest patches must be applied,
- attacks must be isolated and quarantined and
- affected components must be able to be healed.

Orchestration

The centralized nature of cloud computing enables access to a scalable and elastic pool of shareable physical or virtual resources. As computing is distributed to the edge, resources can still be shareable, but elasticity is challenged because:

- compute resources could be in separate islands where they cannot communicate to coordinate computation,
- locations of compute resources may be difficult or costly to access,
- compute in ruggedized enclosures might not be expandable and
- technicians to perform the work may not be easily available at the edge.

With these limitations, the approach is inverted. Understanding both the "as-built" compute target and net-available resources is critical to deploying the right software to the right location. Once deployed, tools to manage, monitor and secure the entire lifecycle are required. Software may need to be throttled or redeployed, memory usage restricted, databases and logs truncated if resource thresholds are challenged. We also need to predict usage trends to address issues before they occur.

The challenge for developers and administrators is to understand not only the physical requirements of their applications (computing inputs, outputs, connectivity, etc.), but also the security and processing requirements and how those requirements translate to different CPU and OS types. Industry standard calculations and metrics may be required.

The two main activities essential to deliver an orchestration solution are:

- infrastructure management to handle the lifecycle of devices at the edge including the commissioning and provisioning of resources and
- orchestration to manage the lifecycle of services and applications and the dependencies between them.

Various standardization efforts share this understanding of orchestration, such as the ETSI Multi-Access Edge Computing (MEC) initiative, the ETSI NFV Management and Orchestration (MANO).

Orchestration and infrastructure management at the edge poses challenges not faced in the cloud mainly due to:

Heterogeneity of devices and application domains: At the edge, there are no expectations on homogeneity regarding devices, or the hardware and software platforms. An infrastructure management system needs to be flexible enough to manage a plethora of devices to consume their resources seamlessly. To provide some level of homogeneity at the edge, both virtualization and containerization technologies may be employed. Also, devices can behave differently based on the application domain. An orchestration solution in a smart factory environment where the nodes are static and the network reliable will have a different behaviour from those orchestrating a logistics or smart cities domain where vehicles are consistently mobile and subjected to variable connection quality.

Different connectivity and communication technologies: IIoT gateways must handle multiple connectivity solutions using different protocols. The orchestrator must be aware of the available solutions to guarantee communication between deployed functions and applications.

Differences in capabilities, requirements and constraints: The higher level of homogeneity and the virtually infinite availability of resources in the cloud ease the orchestration process. Conversely, a broader range of service requirements, device capabilities and constraints are observed at the edge. For example, devices at the edge have different sensors, actuators, real-time operating system or networks; some nodes can provide accelerators, others will not. The orchestrator must be aware of the capabilities found in the infrastructure. Also, the constraints on these nodes need to be known beforehand (e.g. bandwidth, battery, CPU power, memory). At orchestration time, a service must be able to describe its requirements, and the requirements will be checked against the available capabilities and constraints found in the infrastructure.

With that in mind, orchestrators can operate both vertically and horizontally. Vertical orchestrators handle services in a specific domain, while horizontal orchestrators manage services across different domains providing integration among them. An example would be a smart factory that relies on a logistics company, and each has its own orchestrator. A horizontal orchestrator composes services that span the different domains (e.g. a service that adjusts throughput of a production line based on the current location of the necessary supplies).

Orchestration is an important aspect of edge computing to provide a platform to support both IT and OT activities in IIoT. The ability to coordinate the deployment of new services and applications gives the edge the capacity to be programmable and deliver the services required by its consumers. While trying to ensure the quality of the service required, its presence in edge solutions needs to be enforced.

References

[1] Ericsson, *Hyperscale cloud – reimagining data centres from hardware to applications*, May 2016 [Online]. Available: http://www.ericsson.com/res/docs/whitepapers/wp-hyperscale-cloud.pdf. [Accessed 19 September 2017].

[2] SATYANARAYANAN, M., *The Emergence of Edge Computing*, IEE Computer, Vol. 50, pp. 30–39, January 2017.

[3] International Data Corporation, *IDC FutureScape: Worldwide Internet of Things 2017 Predictions*, November 2016 [Online]. Available: https://www.idc.com/getdoc.jsp?containerId=US40755816. [Accessed 19 September 2017].

[4] SIMSEK, M. et al., *5G-Enabled Tactile Internet*, IEEE Journal on Selected Areas in Communications, Vol. 34 (No. 3), March 2016.

[5] ITU-T, *The Tactile Internet*, International Telecommunication Union, August 2014.

[6] IEC, *Factory of the Future,* White Paper, 2017 [Online]. Available: http://www.iec.ch/whitepaper/ futurefactory. [Accessed 19 September 2017].

[7] Mitsubishi Electric, *e-F@ctory*, 2017 [Online]. Available: http://sg.mitsubishielectric.com/fa/en/ download_files/solutions/e_Factory.pdf. [Accessed 19 September 2017].

[8] PLAN.ONE, *PLAT.One Platform*, 2017 [Online]. Available: https://www.sap.com/products/iot-platform-cloud.html. [Accessed 19 September 2017].

[9] 5G-PPP, *5G Automotive Vision,* October 2015 [Online]. Available: https://5g-ppp.eu/wp-content/ uploads/2014/02/5G-PPP-White-Paper-on-Automotive-Vertical-Sectors.pdf. [Accessed 19 September 2017].

[10] European Commission, *European strategy on Cooperative Intelligent Transport Systems (C-ITS)*, 30 November 2016 [Online]. Available: https://ec.europa.eu/transport/themes/its/c-its_en. [Accessed 19 September 2017].

[11] European Commission, *5G for Europe: An Action Plan*, 14 September 2016 [Online]. Available: ec.europa.eu/newsroom/dae/document.cfm?doc_id=17131. [Accessed 19 September 2017].

[12] IEEE 802.11p-2010, *IEEE Standard for Information technology – Local and metropolitan area networks – Specific requirements – Part 11: Wireless LAN Medium Access Control (MAC) and Physical Layer (PHY) Specifications, Amendment 6: Wireless Access in Vehicular Environments.* 15 July 2010 [Online]. Available: https://standards.ieee.org/findstds/standard/802.11p-2010.html. [Accessed 19 September 2017].

[13] DOKIC, J., MÜLLER, B., MEYER, G., *European Roadmap: Smart Systems for Automated Driving,* European Technology Platform on Smart Systems Integration (EPoSS), April 2015, [Online]. Available: http://www.smart-systems-integration.org/public/documents/publications/EPoSS%20 Roadmap_Smart%20Systems%20for%20Automated%20Driving_V2_April%202015.pdf. [Accessed 19 September 2017].

[14] Dedicated Short-Range Communications (DSRC) Fact Sheet, Intelligent Transport Systems Joint Program Office, U.S. Department of Transportation [Online]. Available: http://www.its.dot.gov/ factsheets/pdf/JPO-034_DSRC.pdf. [Accessed 19 September 2017].

[15] 5G Americas, *V2X Cellular Solutions*, October 2016 [Online]. Available: http://www.5gamericas.org/files/2914/7769/1296/5GA_V2X_Report_FINAL_for_upload.pdf. [Accessed 19 September 2017].

[16] BEDO, J-S., CALVANESE STRINATI, E., CASTELLVI, S., CHERIF, T., FRASCOLLA, V., HAERICK, W., KORTHALS, I., LAZARO, O., SUTEDJO, E., USATORRE, L., WOLLSCHLAEGER, M., *5G and the Factories of the Future.* 5G-PPP White Paper, 2015 [Online]. Available: https://5g-ppp.eu/wp-content/uploads/2014/02/5G-PPP-White-Paper-on-Factories-of-the-Future-Vertical-Sector.pdf. [Accessed 19 September 2017].

[17] KOTT, A., SWAMI, A., WEST, B. J., *The Internet of Battle Things*, IEEE Computer, vol. 49, p. 70-75, December 2016.

[18] *Proximity-based services (ProSe); Stage 2,* TR 23.303 3GPP; December 2016 [Online]. Available: https://portal.3gpp.org/desktopmodules/Specifications/SpecificationDetails.aspx?specificationId= 840.[Accessed 19 September 2017].

[19] GOODYEAR, M., LOUIS, J.H., *Defining the Security Domain,* University of Kansas, 2015 [Online]. Available: http://slideplayer.com/slide/2353814. [Accessed 19 September 2017].

[20] 5G-Ensure, *5G Security Architecture* [Online]. Available: http://www.5gensure.eu/5g-ensure-architecture. [Accessed 19 September 2017].

[21] Global Platform, *Internet of Things White Paper,* May 2014 [Online]. Available: https://www.globalplatform.org/documents/whitepapers/IoT_public_whitepaper_v1.0.pdf. [Accessed 19 September 2017].

[22] ANCUTA CORICI, A., EMMELMANN, M., LUO, J., SHRESTHA, R., CORICI, M., MAGEDANZ, T., *IoT inter-security domain trust transfer and service dispatch solution,* 2016 IEEE 3rd World Forum on Internet of Things (WF-IoT), December 2016.

[23] TAPSCOTT, D., TAPSCOTT, A., *Blockchain Revolution: How the Technology Behind Bitcoin Is Changing Money, Business, and the World*, Portfolio, Penguin Random House, New York, 2016.

[24] SWAN, M., *Blockchain: Blueprint for a new economy*, O'Reilly Media, Sebastopol, California, 2015.

[25]　SZABO, N., *The Idea of Smart Contracts*, [Online]. Available: http://www.fon.hum.uva.nl/rob/ Courses/InformationInSpeech/CDROM/Literature/LOTwinterschool2006/szabo.best.vwh.net/idea. html. [Accessed 19 September 2017].

[26]　SWANSON, T., *Consensus-as-a-service: a brief report on the emergence of permissioned, distributed ledger systems*, 6 April 2015 [Online]. Available: http://www.ofnumbers.com/wp-content/ uploads/2015/04/Permissioned-distributed-ledgers.pdf. [Accessed 19 September 2017].

[27]　ANTONOPOULOS, A.M., *Mastering Bitcoin: Unlocking Digital Cryptocurrencies*, O'Reilly Media, Sebastopol, California, 2015.

[28]　SIGNORIN, M., *Towards an internet of trust: issues and solutions for identification and authentication in the internet of things*, University Pompeu Fabra, Barcelona, Spain, 2015.

[29]　IBM, *Empowering the edge: Practical insights on a decentralized Internet of Things*. April 2015 [Online]. Available: https://www-935.ibm.com/services/multimedia/GBE03662USEN.pdf. [Accessed 19September 2017].

[30]　GOTTHOLD, K., ECKERT, D., *Deutschland erkennt Bitcoin als "privates Geld*. Welt N24 16, August 2013 [Online]. Available: https://www.welt.de/finanzen/geldanlage/article119086297/Deutschland-erkennt-Bitcoin-als-privates-Geld-an.html. [Accessed 19 September 2017].

[31]　PETERS, M., *Software-Defined Storage: A Buzzword Worth Examining*, 18 January 2013 NetworkComputing.com [Online]. Available: http://www.networkcomputing.com/ storage/software-defined-storage-buzzword-worth-examining/1334995080

Printed in Great Britain
by Amazon